1997

If you're a teenager or you know one (or two!), this is the book for you!

You could be *Armed and Dangerous! Armed . . .* with the Word of God, the best weapon to confront the forces of Satan at work in our world.

Dangerous . . . because you posses knowledge that could change attitudes, hearts, and maybe the world! This book will help you find the answers to today's tough topics from abortion to war from the most reliable source . . . God's Word!

" All Scripture is God-breathed and is useful for teaching, rebuking, correcting & training in righteousness, so that the man of God may be thoroughly equipped for every good work."

2 Timothy 3: 16-17

armed AND *dangerous*

STRAIGHT ANSWERS FROM THE BIBLE

compiled
by Ken Abraham

A BARBOUR BOOK

All Scripture quotations are from the Authorized King James Version of the Bible unless otherwise noted.

Scripture quotations marked (NIV) are taken from the HOLY BIBLE, NEW INTERNATIONAL VERSION®. NIV®. Copyright © 1973, 1978, 1984 by International Bible Society. Used by permission of Zondervan Publishing House. All rights reserved.

© 1991 by Ken Abraham

All rights reserved. No part of this publication may be reproduced or transmitted in any form or by any means without written permission of the publisher.

Trade paper ISBN 1-55748-242-X
Leatherette (Inspirational Library) ISBN 1-55748-241-1

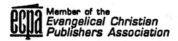

Member of the
Evangelical Christian
Publishers Association

Published by Barbour and Company, Inc.
P.O. Box 719
Uhrichsville, Ohio 44683

Typeset by Typetronix, Inc., Fort Myers, Florida

Printed in the United States of America

CONTENTS

INTRODUCTION ix
- Abortion 1
- Abuse 4
- Accountability 7
- Adultery 9
- Alcohol 11
- Ambition 14
- Anger 15
- Anxiety 17
- Appearance 20
- Assurance 22
- Astrology 25
- Attitude 27
- Backsliding 29
- Bad habits 31
- Baptism 33
- Beauty 37
- Bitterness 40

Contents

Born again (how to be) 42
Church 48
Clothes 50
Compassion 52
Conceit 54
Confession 56
Confidence 59
Conformity 61
Courage 63
Criticism 65
Cults 67
Dancing 70
Dating 72
Death 74
Deceit 77
Defeat 79
Demons 81
Depression 84
Discouragement 86
Divorce 88
Doubt 90
Drug abuse 92
Enemies 94
Envy 96
Faith 98
Fame 100

Fear 102
Flattery 104
Forgiveness 106
Friends 109
The Future 111
Gambling 113
Gifts from God 115
Giving 118
Goals 120
Gossip 122
Grief 124
Guilt 126
Healing 129
Heaven 132
Hell 135
Home 138
Homosexuality 140
Honesty 142
Humility 144
Hypocrisy 146
Incest 149
Laziness 152
Loneliness 154
Love 156
Loyalty 159
Lust 161

Contents

Marriage 164
Miracles 167
Money 170
Music 173
Obedience 175
The Occult 178
Parents 181
Patience 183
Peace 185
Peer pressure 187
Persecution 189
Pornography 191
Prayer 193
Pride 196
Prophecy 198
Punishment 201
Respect 203
Restitution 205
Resurrection 207
Revenge 209
Salvation 211
Satan 213
Self-control 216
Self-image 218
Self-pity 220
Sexual immorality 222

Shame 224
Talents 226
Temptation 228
Thankfulness 231
Thoughts 233
Trouble 235
Trust 238
Unpardonable sin 240
War 242
Will of God (how to find, know, and obey) 243
Wisdom 247
Witnessing 249
Work 252
Worship 254

Introduction

Most of us have spent a lot of time flipping through the pages of the Bible, looking for what God's Word says about a certain subject. It's frustrating when you can't find the information you are looking for: "I know the Bible talks about this issue someplace; I just can't figure out where!" Many students get discouraged and give up the search without satisfaction.

Armed and Dangerous is the antidote for frustration! Many key verses of Scripture that relate to the compelling issues of our time—topics such as *abortion, cults, homosexuality, self-image, lust, demons, war,* and many more—are contained in this one compact volume. In addition, you will find the usual subjects included in most Bible "promise" books.

Because the Scriptures are arranged topically, you can use *Armed and Dangerous* as a study guide, reference resource, or devotional aid in your own walk with God.

When you need straight answers—straight from the Bible—turn to *Armed and Dangerous*, God's Word for your contemporary condition.

Ken Abraham

abortion.

And God said, Let us make man in our image, after our likeness .... *Genesis 1:26*

Thou shalt not kill.
Exodus 20:13; Deuteronomy 5:17

I praise you because I am fearfully and wonderfully made; your works are wonderful, I know that full well. My frame was not hidden from you when I was made in the secret place. When I was woven together in the depths of the earth, your eyes saw my unformed body. All the days ordained for me were written in your book before one of them came to be. *Psalm 139:14-16* (NIV)

Can a woman forget her sucking child, that she should not have compassion on the son of her womb? yea, they may forget, yet will I not forget thee. *Isaiah 49:15*

Before I formed thee in the belly I knew thee; and before thou camest forth out of the womb I sanctified thee, and I ordained thee a prophet unto the nations.   *Jeremiah 1:5*

Children are an heritage of the Lord: and the fruit of the womb is his reward.   *Psalm 127:3*

There is a way that seemeth right unto a man, but the end thereof are the ways of death.
Proverbs 16:25

And it came to pass, that, when Elisabeth heard the salutation of Mary, the babe leaped in her womb; and Elisabeth was filled with the Holy Ghost.   *Luke 1:41*

But when it pleased God, who separated me from my mother's womb, and called me by his grace . . . .
Galatians 1:15

Forgiveness for Aborting a Baby

Wash you, make you clean; put away the evil of your doings from before mine eyes; cease to do evil; learn to do well; seek judgment, relieve the oppressed, judge the fatherless, plead for the widow. Come now, and let us reason together, saith the

LORD; though your sins be as scarlet, they shall be as white as snow; though they be red like crimson, they shall be as wool.   *Isaiah 1:16-13*

If we confess our sins, he is faithful and just to forgive us our sins, and to cleanse us from all unrighteousness.   *1 John 1:9*

Let the wicked forsake his way, and the unrighteous man his thoughts: and let him return unto the Lord, and he will have mercy upon him; and to our God for he will abundantly pardon.   *Isaiah 55:7*

But if we walk in the light as he is in the light, we have fellowship one with another, and the blood of Jesus Christ his Son cleanseth us from all sin.
1 John 1:7

And Jesus said unto her, Neither do I condemn thee: go, and sin no more.   *John 8:11*

ABUSE.

For the Abused Person

Come unto me, all ye that labor and are heavy laden, and I will give you rest.   *Matthew 11:28*

"I sought the Lord and he answered me; he delivered me from all my fears. Those who look to him are radiant; their faces are never covered with shame."
Psalm 34:4, 5 (NIV)

Casting all your care upon him; for he careth for you.   *1 Peter 5:7*

Thou wilt keep him in perfect peace, whose mind is stayed on thee: because he trusteth in thee. Trust ye in the LORD for ever: for in the LORD JEHOVAH is everlasting strength.   *Isaiah 26: 4, 5*

Trust in the Lord with all thine heart; and lean not unto thine own understanding. In all thy ways

acknowledge him, and he shall direct thy paths.
Proverbs 3:5, 6

Why are you downcast, O my soul? Why so disturbed within me? Put your hope in God, for I will yet praise him, my Savior and my God.
Psalm 42:11 (NIV)

For the Abusive Person

Husbands, love your wives, even as Christ also loved the church, and gave himself for it . . . . So ought men to love their wives as their own bodies. He that loveth his wife loveth himself. For no man ever yet hated his own flesh; but nourisheth it and cherisheth it, even as the Lord the church.
Ephesians 5:25, 28, 29

Do not be deceived: Neither the sexually immoral nor idolaters nor male prostitutes nor homosexual offenders nor thieves nor the greedy nor drunkards nor slanderers nor swindlers will inherit the kingdom of God. And that is what some of you were. But you were washed, you were sanctified, you were justified in the name of the Lord Jesus Christ and by the Spirit of our God.
1 Corinthians 6:9-11 (NIV)

But the fruit of the Spirit is love, joy, peace, longsuffering, gentleness, goodness, faith, meekness, temperance: against such there is no law.
Galatians 5:22, 23

Likewise, ye husbands, dwell with them according to knowledge, giving honor unto the wife, as unto the weaker vessel, and so being heirs together of the grace of life; that your prayers be not hindered.
1 Peter 3:7

accountability.

So then every one of us shall give account of himself to God. *Romans 14:12*

For we are taking pains to do what is right, not only in the eyes of the Lord but also in the eyes of men. *2 Corinthians 8:21* (NIV)

For we must all appear before the judgment seat of Christ; that every one may receive the things done in his body, according to that he hath done, whether it be good or bad. *2 Corinthians 5:10*

Iron sharpeneth iron; so a man sharpeneth the countenance of his friend. *Proverbs 27:17*

But I say unto you, that every idle word that men shall speak, they shall give account thereof in the day of judgment. For by thy words thou shalt be justified, and by thy words thou shalt be condemned. *Matthew 12:36, 37*

8 Accountability

Obey them that have rule over you, and submit yourselves: for they watch for your souls, as they that must give account . . . .   *Hebrews 13:17*

And he said also unto his disciples, there was a certain rich man, which had a steward; and the same was accused unto him that he had wasted his goods. And he called him, and said unto him, How is it that I hear this of thee? give an account of thy stewardship . . . .   *Luke 16:1, 2*

"When I say to the wicked, 'O wicked man, you will surely die,' and you do not speak out to dissuade him from his ways, that wicked man will die for his sin, and I will hold you accountable for his blood. But if you do warn the wicked man to turn from his ways and he does not do so, he will die for his sin, but you will have saved yourself."
Ezekiel 33:8, 9 (NIV)

adultery.

Thou shalt not commit adultery. *Exodus 20:14*

" 'If a man commits adultery with another man's wife—with the wife of his neighbor—both the adulterer and the adulteress must be put to death.' "
Leviticus 20:10 (NIV)

But a man who commits adultery lacks judgment; whoever does so destroys himself.
Proverbs 6:32 (NIV)

Ye have heard that it was said by them of old time, Thou shalt not commit adultery: but I say unto you, that whosoever looketh on a woman to lust after her hath committed adultery with her already in his heart. *Matthew 5:27, 28*

Whosoever putteth away his wife, and marrieth another, committeth adultery: and whosoever marrieth her that is put away from her husband committeth adultery. *Luke 16:18*

10   Adultery

And if a woman shall put away her husband, and be married to another, she committeth adultery.
Mark 10:12

Know ye not that the unrighteous shall not inherit the kingdom of God? Be not deceived: neither fornicators, nor idolaters, nor adulterers, nor effeminate, nor abusers of themselves with mankind . . . shall inherit the kingdom of God.
1 Corinthians 6:9, 10

Marriage is honourable in all, and the bed undefiled: but whoremongers and adulterers God will judge.
Hebrews 13:4

For out of the heart proceed evil thoughts, murders, adulteries, fornications, thefts, false witness, blasphemies . . . .   *Matthew 15:19*

He that covereth his sins shall not prosper: but whoso confesseth and forsaketh them shall have mercy.   *Proverbs 28:13*

If we confess our sins, he is faithful and just to forgive us our sins, and to cleanse us from all unrighteousness.   *1 John 1:9*

. . . Jesus said unto her, Neither do I condemn thee: go, and sin no more.   *John 8:11*

ALCOHOL.

Wine is a mocker, strong drink is raging: and whosoever is deceived thereby is not wise.
Proverbs 20:1

... He that loveth wine and oil shall not be rich.
Proverbs 21:17

Do not join those who drink too much wine or gorge themselves on meat, for drunkards and gluttons become poor.... *Proverbs 23:20, 21* (NIV)

Woe unto them that rise up early in the morning, that they may follow strong drink; that continue until night, till wine inflame them. *Isaiah 4:11*

Who hath woe? who hath sorrow? who hath contentions? who hath babblings? who hath wounds without cause? who hath redness of eyes? they that tarry long at the wine; they that go to seek mixed wine. *Proverbs 23:29, 30*

Be careful, or your hearts will be weighed down with dissipation, drunkenness, and the anxieties of life, and that day will close on you unexpectedly like a trap. *Luke 21:34* (NIV)

Let us walk honestly, as in the day; not in rioting and drunkenness . . . . *Romans 13:13*

Do you not know that the wicked will not inherit the kingdom of God? Do not be deceived: Neither the sexually immoral nor idolaters nor adulterers nor male prostitutes nor homosexual offenders nor thieves nor the greedy nor drunkards nor slanderers nor swindlers will inherit the kingdom of God.
1 Corinthians 6:9, 10 (NIV)

Envyings, murders, drunkenness, revellings, and such like: of the which I tell you before, as I have also told you in time past, that they which do such things shall not inherit the kingdom of God.
Galatians 5:21

And be not drunk with wine, wherein is excess, but be filled with the Spirit . . . . *Ephesians 5:18*

Therefore if any man be in Christ, he is a new creature: old things are passed away; behold, all things are become new. *2 Corinthians 5:17*

I beseech you therefore, brethren, by the mercies of God, that ye present your bodies a living sacrifice . . . and be not conformed to this world: but be ye transformed by the renewing of your mind, that ye may prove what is that good, and acceptable, and perfect, will of God.   *Romans 12:1, 2*

If the Son therefore shall make you free, ye shall be free indeed.   *John 8:36*

ambition.

Do nothing out of selfish ambition or vain conceit, but in humility consider others better than yourselves.   *Philippians 2:2* (NIV)

For what is a man profited, if he shall gain the whole world, and lose his own soul? or what shall a man give in exchange for his soul?
Matthew 16:26

Make it your ambition to lead a quiet life, to mind your own business and to work with your hands, just as we told you, so that your daily life may win the respect of outsiders and so that you will not be dependent on anybody.
1 Thessalonians 4:11, 12 (NIV)

For where you have envy and selfish ambition, there you find disorder and every evil practice.
James 3:16 (NIV)

anger.

A fool gives full vent to his anger, but a wise man keeps himself under control. *Proverbs 29:11* (NIV)

He that is soon angry dealeth foolishly: and a man of wicked devices is hated. *Proverbs 14:17*

He that is slow to wrath is of great understanding, but he that is hasty of spirit exalteth folly.
Proverbs 14:29

Cease from anger, and forsake wrath: fret not thyself in any wise to do evil. *Psalm 37:8*

A wrathful man stirreth up strife: but he that is slow to anger appeaseth strife. *Proverbs 15:18*

Ye have heard that it was said by them of old time, Thou shalt not kill; and whosoever shall kill shall be in danger of the judgment: But I say unto you, that whosoever is angry with his brother without a cause shall be in danger of the judgment . . . .
Matthew 5:21, 22

16　Anger

A soft answer turneth away wrath: but grievous words stir up anger.　*Proverbs 15:1*

Be ye angry, and sin not: let not the sun go down upon your wrath: Neither give place to the devil.
Ephesians 4:26, 27

Let all bitterness, and wrath, and anger, and clamour, and evil speaking, be put away from you, with all malice . . . .　*Ephesians 4:31*

Make no friendship with an angry man; and with a furious man thou shalt not go: Lest thou learn his ways, and get a snare to thy soul.
Proverbs 22:24, 25

ANXIETY.

Humble yourselves therefore under the mighty hand of God, that he may exalt you in due time: Casting all your care upon him; for he careth for you.   *1 Peter 5:6, 7*

Thou wilt keep him in perfect peace, whose mind is stayed on thee: because he trusteth in thee.
Isaiah 26:3

Trust in the Lord with all thine heart; and lean not unto thine own understanding. In all thy ways acknowledge him, and he shall direct thy paths.
Proverbs 3:5, 6

Blessed is the man that trusteth in the Lord, and whose hope the Lord is. For he shall be as a tree planted by the waters, and that spreadeth out her roots by the river, and shall not see when heat cometh, but her leaf shall be green; and shall not be careful in the year of drought, neither shall cease from yielding fruit.   *Jeremiah 17:7, 8*

18 Anxiety

Therefore I tell you, do not worry about your life, what you will eat or drink; or about your body, what you will wear. Is not life more important than food, and the body more important than clothes? . . . So do not worry, saying, 'What shall we eat?' or 'What shall we drink?' or 'What shall we wear?' . . . But seek first his kingdom and his righteousness, and all these things will be given to you as well. Therefore do not worry about tomorrow, for tomorrow will worry about itself. Each day has enough trouble of its own.   *Matthew 6:25, 31, 33, 34* (NIV)

Why art thou cast down, O my soul? and why art thou disquieted within me? hope thou in God: for I shall yet praise him, who is the health of my countenance, and my God.   *Psalm 42:11*

I sought the Lord, and He heard me, and delivered me from all my fears.   *Psalm 34:4*

Cast thy burden upon the Lord, and he shall sustain thee: he shall never suffer the righteous to be moved.   *Psalm 55:22*

Do not be anxious about anything, but in everything, by prayer and petition, with thanksgiving, present your requests to God. And the peace of God, which transcends all understanding, will guard your hearts and minds in Christ Jesus.
Philippians 4:6, 7 (NIV)

And we know that all things work together for good to them that love God, to them who are the called according to his purpose. *Romans 8:28*

But my God shall supply all your need according to his riches in glory by Christ Jesus.
Philippians 4:19

appearance.

Judge not according to the appearance, but judge righteous judgment.   *John 7:24*

... The Lord seeth not as man seeth; for man looketh on the outward appearance, but the LORD looketh on the heart.   *1 Samuel 16:7*

For we commend not ourselves again unto you, but give you occasion to glory on our behalf, that ye may have somewhat to answer them which glory in appearance, and not in heart.
2 Corinthians 5:12

Your beauty should not come from outward adornment, such as braided hair and the wearing of gold jewelry and fine clothes. Instead, it should be that of your inner self, the unfading beauty of a gentle and quiet spirit, which is of great worth in God's sight.   *1 Peter 3:3, 4* (NIV)

... God does not judge by external appearance ....   *Galatians 2:6* (NIV)

Moreover when ye fast, be not as the hypocrites, of a sad countenance: for they disfigure their faces, that they may appear unto men to fast. Verily I say unto you, they have their reward.   *Matthew 6:16*

Abstain from all appearance of evil.
1 Thessalonians 5:22

assurance.

He that believeth on the Son hath everlasting life: and he that believeth not the Son shall not see life; but the wrath of God abideth on him. *John 3:36*

He that hath the Son hath life: and he that hath not the Son of God hath not life. These things I have written unto you that believe on the name of the Son of God; that ye may know that ye have eternal life, and that ye may believe on the name of the Son of God. *1 John 5:12, 13*

. . . According to the eternal purpose which he purposed in Christ Jesus our Lord: In whom we have boldness and access with confidence by the faith of him. *Ephesians 3:11, 12*

We know that we have passed from death unto life, because we love the brethren. He that loveth not his brother abideth in death. *1 John 3:14*

And hereby we know that we are of the truth, and shall assure our hearts before him. For if our heart

condemn us, God is greater than our heart, and knoweth all things. Beloved, if our heart condemn us not, then have we confidence toward God.
1 John 3:19-21

Let us draw near with a true heart in full assurance of faith, having our hearts sprinkled from an evil conscience, and our bodies washed with pure water. *Hebrews 10:22*

For I know that my redeemer liveth, and that he shall stand at the latter day upon the earth: And though after my skin worms destroy this body, yet in my flesh shall I see God: Whom I shall see for myself, and mine eyes shall behold, and not another . . . . *Job 19:25-27*

But know that the Lord hath set apart him that is godly for himself: the Lord will hear when I call unto him. *Psalm 4:3*

The Spirit himself testifies with our spirit that we are God's children. *Romans 8:16* (NIV)

For I am persuaded, that neither death, nor life, nor angels, nor principalities, nor powers, nor things present, nor things to come, nor height, nor depth, nor any other creature, shall be able to separate us from the love of God, which is in Christ Jesus our Lord. *Romans 8:38, 39*

Assurance

... I am not ashamed: for I know whom I have believed, and am persuaded that he is able to keep that which I have committed unto him against that day. *2 Timothy 1:12*

ASTROLOGY.

Therefore shall evil come upon thee; thou shalt not know from whence it riseth: and mischief shall fall upon thee; thou shalt not be able to put it off: and desolation shall come upon thee suddenly, which thou shalt not know. Stand now with thine enchantments, and with the multitude of thy sorceries, wherein thou hast laboured from thy youth . . . Let now the astrologers, the stargazers, the monthly prognosticators, stand up, and save thee from these things that shall come upon thee. Behold, they shall be as stubble; the fire shall burn them; they shall not deliver themselves from the power of the flame: there shall not be a coal to warm at, nor fire to sit before it.   *Isaiah 47:11-14*

If there be found among you . . . man or woman, that hath wrought wickedness in the sight of the LORD thy God, in transgressing his covenant, and hath gone and served other gods, and worshipped them, either the sun, or moon, or any of the host of heaven, which I have not commanded . . . Then

shalt thou bring forth that man or woman, which have committed that wicked thing . . . and shalt stone them with stones, till they die.
Deuteronomy 17:2, 3, 5

There shall not be found among you anyone that maketh his son or his daughter to pass through the fire, or that useth divination, or an observer of times, or an enchanter, or a witch. Or a charmer, or a consulter with familiar spirits, or a wizard, or a necromancer. For all that do these things are an abomination unto the LORD:
Deuteronomy 18:10-12

Thou shalt have no other gods before me. Thou shall not make unto thee any graven image, or any likeness of any thing that is in heaven above, or that is in the earth beneath or that is in the water under the earth: *Exodus 20:3, 4*

attitude.

Your attitude should be the same as that of Christ Jesus . . . .   *Philippians 2:5* (NIV)

Therefore, since Christ suffered in his body, arm yourselves also with the same attitude, because he who has suffered in his body is done with sin. As a result, he does not live the rest of his earthly life for evil human desires, but rather for the will of God.   *1 Peter 4:1, 2* (NIV)

You were taught, with regard to your former way of life, to put off your old self, which is being corrupted by its deceitful desire; to be made new in the attitude of your mind; and to put on the new self, created to be like God in true righteousness and holiness.   *Ephesians 4:22-24* (NIV)

And herein do I exercise myself, to have a good conscience void of offense toward God, and toward men.   *Acts 24:16*

28   Attitude

Lie not to one another, seeing that ye have put off the old man with his deeds; and have put on the new man which is renewed in knowledge after the image of him that created him.
Colossians 3:9, 10

And whatsoever ye do in word or deed, do all in the name of the Lord Jesus, giving thanks to God and the Father by him.   *Colossians 3:17*

For the word of God is quick, and powerful, and sharper than any two edged sword, piercing even to the dividing asunder of soul and spirit . . . and is a discerner of the thoughts and intents of the heart.   *Hebrews 4:12*

And let the peace of God rule in your hearts, to the which also ye are called in one body; and be ye thankful.   *Colossians 3:15*

backsliding.

The backslider in heart shall be filled with his own ways . . . .   *Proverbs 14:14*

. . . Surely these are poor; they are foolish: for they know not the way of the Lord, nor the judgment of their God. I will get me unto the great men, and will speak unto them; for they have known the way of the LORD, and the judgment of their God: but these have altogether broken the yoke, and burst the bonds . . . Because their transgressions are many, and their backslidings are increased.
Jeremiah 5:4-6

Thou hast forsaken me, saith the LORD, thou art gone backward: therefore I will stretch out my hand against thee, and destroy thee; I am weary with repenting . . . since they return not from their ways.
Jeremiah 15:6, 7

Yea, they turned back and tempted God, and limited the Holy One of Israel.   *Psalm 78:41*

Backsliding

Nevertheless I have somewhat against thee, because thou hast left thy first love. Remember therefore from whence thou art fallen, and repent, and do the first works; or else I will come unto thee quickly, and I will remove thy candlestick out of his place, except thou repent.   *Revelation 2:4, 5*

I will save them from all their sinful backsliding, and I will cleanse them. They will be my people, and I will be their God.   *Ezekiel 37:23* (NIV)

BAD HABITS.

The acts of the sinful nature are obvious: sexual immorality, impurity and debauchery; idolatry and witchcraft; hatred, discord, jealousy, fits of rage, selfish ambition, dissensions, factions and envy; drunkenness, orgies, and the like. I warn you, as I did before, that those who live like this will not inherit the kingdom of God.
Galatians 5:19-21 (NIV)

He that hath a froward heart findeth no good: and he that hath a perverse tongue falleth into mischief.
Proverbs 17:20

The lip of truth shall be established for ever: but a lying tongue is but for a moment. Deceit is in the heart of them that imagine evil: but to the counsellors of peace is joy . . . Lying lips are abomination to the LORD: but they that deal truly are his delight.   *Proverbs 12:19, 20, 22*

Bad Habits

Live such good lives among the pagans that, though they accuse you of doing wrong, they may see your good deeds and glorify God on the day he visits us.   *1 Peter 2:12* (NIV)

Thy word have I hid in mine heart, that I might not sin against thee.   *Psalm 119:11*

Submit yourselves therefore to God. Resist the devil, and he will flee from you.   *James 4:7*

Do all things without murmurings and disputings: That ye may be blameless and harmless, the sons of God, without rebuke, in the midst of a crooked and perverse nation, among whom ye shine as lights in the world . . . .   *Philippians 2:14, 15*

But shun profane and vain babblings: for they will increase unto more ungodliness.
2 Timothy 2:16

baptism.

In those days came John the Baptist, preaching in the wilderness of Judea, and saying, Repent ye: for the kingdom of heaven is at hand . . . I indeed baptize you with water unto repentance: but he that cometh after me is mightier than I, whose shoes I am not worthy to bear: he shall baptize you with the Holy Ghost, and with fire . . . .
Matthew 3:1, 2, 11

Then cometh Jesus from Galilee to Jordan unto John, to be baptized of him. But John forbad him, saying, I have need to be baptized of thee, and comest thou to me? And Jesus answering said unto him, Suffer it to be so now: for thus it becometh us to fulfil all righteousness. Then he suffered him.
Matthew 3:13, 14, 15

John answered them, saying, I baptize with water: but there standeth one among you, whom ye know not . . . The next day John seeth Jesus coming unto him, and saith, Behold the Lamb of God, which taketh away the sin of the world.   *John 1:26, 29*

... Jesus made and baptized more disciples than John, (though Jesus himself baptized not, but his disciples) ....   *John 4:1, 2*

Then Peter said unto them, Repent, and be baptized every one of you in the name of Jesus Christ for the remission of sins, and ye shall receive the gift of the Holy Ghost.   *Acts 2:38*

Then Ananias went to the house and entered it. Placing his hands on Saul, he said, "Brother Saul, the Lord—Jesus, who appeared to you on the road as you were coming here—has sent me so that you may see again and be filled with the Holy Spirit." Immediately, something like scales fell from Saul's eyes, and he could see again. He got up and was baptized ....   *Acts 9:17, 18* (NIV)

"Can anyone keep these people from being baptized with water? They have received the Holy Spirit just as we have."   *Acts 10:47, 48* (NIV)

And he took them the same hour of the night, and washed their stripes; and was baptized, he and all his, straightway.   *Acts 16:33*

And Crispus, the chief ruler of the synagogue, believed on the Lord with all his house; and many of the Corinthians hearing believed, and were baptized. *Acts 18:8*

Then said Paul, John verily baptized with the baptism of repentance, saying unto the people, that they should believe on him which should come after him, that is, on Christ Jesus. When they heard this, they were baptized in the name of the Lord Jesus. *Acts 19:4, 5*

And now why tarriest thou? arise, and be baptized, and wash away thy sins, calling on the name of the Lord. *Acts 22:16*

Know ye not, that so many of us as were baptized into Jesus Christ were baptized into his death? Therefore we are buried with him by baptism into death: that like as Christ was raised up from the dead by the glory of the Father, even so we also should walk in newness of life. *Romans 6:3, 4*

For by one Spirit we are all baptized into one body . . . and have been all made to drink into one Spirit. *1 Corinthians 12:13*

For ye are all the children of God by faith in Christ Jesus. For as many of you as have been baptized into Christ have put on Christ.
Galatians 3:26, 27

There is one body, and one Spirit, even as ye are called in one hope of your calling; one Lord, one faith, one baptism, one God and Father of all, who is above all, and through all, and in you all.

Ephesians 4:4-6

And this water symbolized baptism that now saves you also—not the removal of dirt from the body but the pledge of a good conscience toward God. It saves you by the resurrection of Jesus Christ.   *1 Peter 3:21* (NIV)

beauty.

Charm is deceptive, and beauty is fleeting; but a woman who fears the LORD is to be praised.
Proverbs 31:30 (NIV)

As a jewel of gold in a swine's snout, so is a fair woman which is without discretion.
Proverbs 11:22

A virtuous woman is a crown to her husband: but she that maketh ashamed is as rottenness in his bones.   *Proverbs 12:4*

Your beauty should not come from outward adornment, such as braided hair and the wearing of gold jewelry and fine clothes. Instead, it should be that of your inner self, the unfading beauty of a gentle and quiet spirit, which is of great worth in God's sight.   *1 Peter 3:3, 4* (NIV)

. . . Rachel was beautiful and well favoured.
Genesis 29:17

... And the name of his wife Abigail: and she was a woman of good understanding, and of a beautiful countenance .... *1 Samuel 25:3*

He hath made every thing beautiful in his time .... *Ecclesiastes 3:11*

How beautiful upon the mountains are the feet of him that bringeth good tidings, that publisheth peace; that bringeth good tidings of good, that publisheth salvation; that saith unto Zion, Thy God reigneth! *Isaiah 52:7*

Woe unto you, scribes and Pharisees, hypocrites! for ye are like unto white sepulchres, which indeed appear beautiful outward, but are within full of dead men's bones, and of all uncleanness.
Matthew 23:27

And let the beauty of the LORD our God be upon us: and establish thou the work of our hands upon us .... *Psalm 90:17*

Give unto the LORD the glory due unto his name; worship the LORD in the beauty of holiness.
Psalm 29:2

The glory of young men is their strength: and the beauty of old men is the grey head. *Proverbs 20:29*

Finally, brethren, whatsoever things are true, whatsoever things are honest, whatsoever things are just, whatsoever things are pure, whatsoever things are of good report; if there be any virtue, and if there be any praise, think on these things.
Philippians 4:8

BITTERNESS.

Let all bitterness, and wrath, and anger, and clamour, and evil speaking, be put away from you, with all malice: and be ye kind to one another, tenderhearted, forgiving one another, even as God for Christ's sake hath forgiven you.
Ephesians 4:31, 32

Therefore, if you are offering your gift at the altar and there remember that your brother has something against you, leave your gift there in front of the altar. First go and be reconciled to your brother; then come and offer your gift.
Matthew 5:23 (NIV)

Bless them which persecute you: bless, and curse not.   *Romans 12:17* (NIV)

Do not repay anyone evil for evil. Be careful to do what is right in the eyes of everybody.
Romans 12:17 (NIV)

... Christ also suffered for us, leaving us an example, that ye should follow his steps ... Who, when he was reviled, reviled not again; when he suffered, he threatened not; but committed himself to him that judgeth righteously . . . .
1 Peter 2:21, 23

Follow peace with all men, and holiness, without which no man shall see the Lord: looking diligently lest any man fail of the grace of God; lest any root of bitterness springing up trouble you, and thereby many be defiled . . . .   *Hebrews 12:14, 15*

Out of the same mouth proceedeth blessing and cursing. My brethren, these things ought not so to be ... But if ye have bitter envying and strife in your hearts, glory not, and lie not against the truth. This wisdom descendeth not from above, but is earthly, sensual, devilish.   *James 3:10, 14, 15*

born again.
(how to be)

For God so loved the world, that he gave his only begotten Son, that whosoever believeth in him should not perish, but have everlasting life.   *John 3:16*

But as many as received him, to them gave he power to become the sons of God, even to them that believe on his name: which were born, not of blood, nor of the will of the flesh, nor of the will of man, but of God.   *John 1:12, 13*

Jesus answered and said unto him, Verily, verily, I say unto thee, Except a man be born again, he cannot see the kingdom of God.   *John 3:3*

That which is born of the flesh is flesh; and that which is born of the Spirit is spirit.   *John 3:6*

For all have sinned, and come short of the glory of God.   *Romans 3:23*

For the wages of sin is death; but the gift of God is eternal life through Jesus Christ our Lord.
Romans 6:23

But God, who is rich in mercy, for his great love wherewith he loved us, even when we were dead in sins, hath quickened us together with Christ . . . For by grace are ye saved through faith; and that not of yourselves: it is the gift of God: not of works, lest any man should boast.
Ephesians 2:4, 5, 8, 9

He himself bore our sins in his body on the tree, so that we might die to sins, and live for righteousness; by his wounds you have been healed.
1 Peter 2:24 (NIV)

Very rarely will anyone die for a righteous man, though for a good man someone might possibly dare to die. But God demonstrates his own love for us in this: While we were yet sinners, Christ died for us.   *Romans 5:7, 8* (NIV)

For God sent not his Son into the world to condemn the world; but that the world through him might be saved. He that believeth on him is not condemned: but he that believeth not is condemned already, because he hath not believed in the name of the only begotten Son of God.   *John 3:17, 18*

There is therefore now no condemnation to them which are in Christ Jesus, who walk not after the flesh, but after the Spirit.   *Romans 8:1*

... Sirs, what must I do to be saved? And they said, Believe on the Lord Jesus Christ, and thou shalt be saved, and thy house.   *Acts 16:30, 31*

Moreover, brethren, I declare unto you the gospel which I preached unto you, which also ye have received, and wherein ye stand; by which also ye are saved, if ye keep in memory what I preached unto you, unless ye have believed in vain.
1 Corinthians 15:1, 2

For I delivered unto you first of all that which I also received, how that Christ died for our sins according to the scriptures; and that he was buried, and that he rose again the third day according to the scriptures . . . .   *1 Corinthians 15:3, 4*

That if thou shalt confess with thy mouth the Lord Jesus, and shalt believe in thine heart that God hath raised him from the dead, thou shalt be saved. For with the heart man believeth unto righteousness; and with the mouth confession is made unto salvation.   *Romans 10:9, 10*

Behold, I stand at the door, and knock: if any man hear my voice, and open the door, I will come in to him, and will sup with him, and he with me.
Revelation 3:20

For the scripture saith, Whosoever believeth on him shall not be ashamed. *Romans 10:11*

Seeing ye have purified your souls in obeying the truth through the Spirit unto unfeigned love of the brethren, see that ye love one another with a pure heart fervently: being born again, not of corruptible seed, but of incorruptible, by the word of God, which liveth and abideth for ever.
1 Peter 1:22, 23

now is the time . . .

If you have never been "born again"—if you have never trusted Jesus Christ as your Savior and invited Him into your life—you can do it right now. If you are not sure you are a Christian, now is the perfect time to make sure.

Look back over the preceding Scriptures and understand that Jesus died for your sins. He defeated death and the devil; He rose again on the third day; He is now alive and well at the right hand of your heavenly Father. Because He lives, you can live too . . . forever with Him in heaven.

Trust the Lord right now and ask Him to save you. Pray something similar to this: "Lord Jesus, I know

You love me, because You proved it by dying on the cross to pay the penalty for my sins. Thank you, Jesus, for doing that for me.

"I admit that I have sinned—against others and against myself, but most of all, against You. Please forgive me for my sins, and give me Your power to resist the temptation to sin.

"I believe that You rose from the dead, and that You really are the only true God. I ask You to come into my life and live at the center of it. Please accept me. By faith, I accept You, Jesus. Thank you for giving me eternal life with You."

If you honestly mean your prayer, Jesus takes you seriously. He causes you to be born again or you could say, born from above.

This is not the end but rather the beginning of a brand-new way of living. Here are four hints that will help you live for Jesus:

> 1. *Tell someone what you have done.* It is important to "go on record" that you have been born again. Tell someone who knows you well enough to notice the difference that Jesus will be making in your life. If you have trouble explaining it, just say something like, "I can't explain all the details yet, but I have committed my life to Jesus Christ and from now on, I'm going to live the way He tells me in His Word."
>
> 2. *Begin reading your Bible.* Start with the *Gospel of John*. Read a bit of the Bible every day.

3. *Pray every day.* Prayer is simply talking to God. He wants to hear from you. Tell Him about your high points and ask Him to help you through the rough spots.

4. *Go to church regularly.* The Church is God's family here on earth. You'll want to be with your church family as frequently as possible for study and service, friendship, and fun.

church.

And I say unto thee, That thou art Peter, and upon this rock I will build my church; and the gates of hell shall not prevail against it.   *Matthew 16:18*

And he is the head of the body, the church: who is the beginning, the firstborn from the dead; that in all things he might have the preeminence.
Colossians 1:18

... Christ is the head of the church: and he is the Saviour of the body ... Christ also loved the church, and gave himself for it.
Ephesians 5:23, 25

For as the body is one, and hath many members, and all the members of that one body, being many, are one body: so also is Christ. For by one Spirit are we all baptized into one body ... and have been all made to drink into one Spirit. For the body is not one member, but many.
1 Corinthians 12:12, 13, 14

... The Lord knoweth them that are his. And, let every one that nameth the name of Christ depart from iniquity.   *2 Timothy 2:19*

And they continued stedfastly in the apostles' doctrine and fellowship, and in breaking of bread, and in prayers.   *Acts 2:42*

Ye also, as living stones, are built up a spiritual house, an holy priesthood, to offer up spiritual sacrifices, acceptable to God by Jesus Christ . . . But ye are a chosen generation, a royal priesthood, an holy nation, a peculiar people, that ye should shew forth the praises of him who hath called you out of darkness into his marvellous light.
1 Peter 2:5, 9

Let us not give up meeting together, as some are in the habit of doing, but let us encourage one another—and all the more as you see the Day approaching.   *Hebrews 10:25* (NIV)

CLOTHES.

A woman must not wear men's clothing, nor a man wear women's clothing, for the LORD your God detests anyone who does this.
Deuteronomy 22:5 (NIV)

I also want women to dress modestly, with decency and propriety, not with braided hair or gold or pearls or expensive clothes, but with good deeds, appropriate for women who profess to worship God.   *1 Timothy 2:9, 10* (NIV)

. . . Take no thought for your life, what ye shall eat; neither for the body, what ye shall put on. The life is more than meat, and the body is more than raiment.   *Luke 12:22, 23*

If you show special attention to the man wearing fine clothes and say, "Here's a good seat for you," but say to the poor man, "You stand there" or "Sit on the floor by my feet," have you not discriminated among yourselves and become judges with evil thoughts? *James 2:3, 4* (NIV)

I put on righteousness, and it clothed me: my judgment was as a robe and a diadem. *Job 29:14*

Beware of false prophets, which come to you in sheep's clothing, but inwardly they are ravening wolves. *Matthew 7:15*

For we brought nothing into this world, and it is certain we can carry nothing out. And having food and raiment let us be therewith content.
1 Timothy 6:7, 8

compassion.

Therefore, as God's chosen people, holy and dearly loved, clothe yourselves with compassion, kindness, humility, gentleness and patience.
Colossians 3:12 (NIV)

And there shall cleave nought of the cursed thing to thine hand: that the LORD may turn from the fierceness of his anger, and shew thee mercy, and have compassion upon thee, and multiply thee, as he hath sworn unto thy fathers . . . .
Deuteronomy 13:17

"This is what the LORD Almighty says: 'Administer true justice; show mercy and compassion to one another. Do not oppress the widow or the fatherless, the alien or the poor. In your hearts do not think evil of each other.' "
Zechariah 7:9, 10 (NIV)

Pure religion and undefiled before God and the Father is this, To visit the fatherless and widows in their affliction, and to keep himself unspotted from the world.   *James 1:27*

He that hath pity upon the poor lendeth unto the LORD; and that which he hath given will he pay him again.   *Proverbs 19:17*

A good man sheweth favour, and lendeth: he will guide his affairs with discretion . . . He hath dispersed, he hath given to the poor; his righteousness endureth for ever; his horn shall be exalted with honour.   *Psalm 112:5, 9*

conceit.

Do nothing out of selfish ambition or vain conceit, but in humility consider others better than yourselves.   *Philippians 2:3* (NIV)

The rich man's wealth is his strong city, and as an high wall in his own conceit. Before destruction the heart of man is haughty, and before honour is humility.   *Proverbs 18:11, 12*

Seest thou a man wise in his own conceit? there is more hope of a fool than of him.   *Proverbs 26:12*

Live in harmony with one another. Do not be proud, but be willing to associate with people of low position. Do not be conceited.
Romans 12:16 (NIV)

Pride goeth before destruction, and an haughty spirit before a fall. Better it is to be of an humble spirit with the lowly, than to divide the spoil with the proud.   *Proverbs 16:18, 19*

Behold, the Lord, the LORD of hosts, shall lop the bough with terror: and the high ones of stature shall be hewn down, and the haughty shall be humbled.   *Isaiah 10:33*

CONFESSION.

I acknowledged my sin unto thee, and mine iniquity have I not hid. I said, I will confess my transgressions unto the LORD; and thou forgavest the iniquity of my sin . . . .   *Psalm 32:5*

If we confess our sins, he is faithful and just to forgive us our sins, and to cleanse us from all unrighteousness.   *1 John 1:9*

He who conceals his sins does not prosper, but whoever confesses and renounces them finds mercy.
Proverbs 28:13

Confess your faults one to another, and pray one for another, that you may be healed. The effectual fervent prayer of a righteous man availeth much.
James 5:16

Whosoever therefore shall confess me before men, him will I confess also before my Father which is in heaven. But whosoever shall deny me before men, him will I also deny before my Father which is in heaven.   *Matthew 10:32, 33*

Nevertheless, God's solid foundation stands firm, sealed with this inscription: "The Lord knows those who are his," and "Everyone who confesses the name of the Lord must turn away from wickedness."   *2 Timothy 2:19* (NIV)

That if thou confess with thy mouth the Lord Jesus, and shalt believe in thine heart that God hath raised him from the dead, thou shalt be saved. For with the heart man believeth unto righteousness; and with the mouth confession is made unto salvation.   *Romans 14:10, 11*

Wherefore God also hath highly exalted him, and given him a name which is above every name: That at the name of Jesus every knee should bow, of things in heaven, and things in earth, and things under the earth; and that every tongue should confess that Jesus Christ is Lord, to the glory of God the Father . . . .   *Philippians 2:9-11*

For many deceivers are entered into the world, who confess not that Jesus Christ is come in the flesh. This is a deceiver and an antichrist.
   2 John 7

Whosoever shall confess that Jesus is the Son of God, God dwelleth in him, and he in God.   *1 John 4:15*

Beloved, believe not every spirit, but try the spirits whether they are of God: because many false prophets are gone out into the world. Hereby know ye the Spirit of God: Every spirit that confesseth that Jesus Christ is come in the flesh is of God: And every spirit that confesseth not that Jesus Christ is come in the flesh is not of God: and this is that spirit of antichrist, whereof ye have heard that it should come; and even now already is it in the world.

1 John 4:1-3

He that overcometh, the same shall be clothed in white raiment; and I will not blot out his name out of the book of life, but I will confess his name before my Father, and before his angels.

Revelation 3:5

confidence.

For we are the circumcision, which worship God in the spirit, and rejoice in Christ Jesus, and have no confidence in the flesh. *Philippians 3:3*

For the LORD shall be thy confidence . . . .
Proverbs 3:26

It is better to trust in the LORD than to put confidence in man. It is better to trust in the LORD than to put confidence in princes.
Psalm 118:8, 9

For you have been my hope, O Sovereign LORD, my confidence since my youth. *Psalm 71:5* (NIV)

In the fear of the LORD is strong confidence: and his children shall have a place of refuge.
Proverbs 14:26

I have confidence in you through the Lord . . . .
Galatians 5:10

Trust ye not in a friend, put ye not confidence in a guide ... For the son dishonoureth the father, the daughter riseth up against her mother, the daughter in law against her mother in law; a man's enemies are the men of his own house. Therefore I will look unto the LORD; I will wait for the God of my salvation; my God will hear me.   *Micah 7:5-7*

For we are made partakers of Christ, if we hold the beginning of our confidence stedfast unto the end.   *Hebrews 3:14*

Cast not away therefore your confidence, which hath great recompence of reward ....
Hebrews 10:35

Beloved, if our heart condemn us not, then have we confidence toward God.   *1 John 3:21*

And this is the confidence that we have in him, that, if we ask any thing according to his will, he heareth us: And if we know that he hear us, whatsoever we ask, we know that we have the petitions that we desired of him.   *1 John 5:14,15*

And now, little children, abide in him; that, when he shall appear, we may have confidence, and not be ashamed before him at his coming.
1 John 2:28

conformity.

I beseech you therefore, brethren, by the mercies of God, that ye present your bodies a living sacrifice, holy, acceptable unto God, which is your reasonable service. And be not conformed to this world: but be ye transformed by the renewing of your mind, that ye may prove what is that good, and acceptable, and perfect will of God.
Romans 12:1, 2

As obedient children, do not conform to the evil desires you had when you lived in ignorance. But just as he who calls you is holy, so be holy in all you do . . . .   *1 Peter 1:14, 15* (NIV)

"And you will know that I am the LORD, for you have not followed my decrees or kept my laws but have conformed to the standards of the nations around you."   *Ezekiel 11:12* (NIV)

Whosoever therefore shall be ashamed of me and of my words in this adulterous and sinful generation; of him also shall the Son of man be ashamed, when he cometh in the glory of his Father with the holy angels.   *Mark 8:38*

Be ye not unequally yoked together with unbelievers: for what fellowship hath righteousness with unrighteousness? and what communion hath light with darkness? ... Wherefore come out from among them, and be ye separate, saith the Lord, and touch not the unclean thing; and I will receive you, and will be a Father unto you, and ye shall be my sons and daughters saith the Lord Almighty.   *2 Corinthians 6:14, 17, 18*

COURAGE.

Be strong and of good courage, fear not, nor be afraid of them: for the LORD thy God, he it is that doth go with thee; he will not fail thee, nor forsake thee.   *Deuteronomy 31:6*

Only be thou strong and very courageous, that thou mayest observe to do according to all the law, which Moses my servant commanded thee: turn not from it to the right hand or to the left, that thou mayest prosper whithersoever thou goest.
Joshua 1:7

"Be strong and let us fight bravely for our people and the cities of our God. The LORD will do what is good in his sight."   *2 Samuel 10:12* (NIV)

Be strong and courageous, be not afraid nor dismayed for the king of Assyria, nor for all the multitude that is with him: for there be more with us than with him: With him is an arm of flesh; but with us is the LORD our God to help us, and to fight our battles . . . .   *2 Chronicles 32:7, 8*

But Jesus immediately said to them: "Take courage! It is I. Don't be afraid."
Matthew 14:27 (NIV)

Now when they saw the boldness of Peter and John, and perceived that they were unlearned and ignorant men, they marvelled; and they took knowledge of them, that they had been with Jesus.   *Acts 4:13*

But Christ is faithful as a son over God's house. And we are his house, if we hold on to our courage and the hope of which we boast.
Hebrews 3:6 (NIV)

criticism.

We want to avoid any criticism of the way we administer this liberal gift . . . .
2 Corinthians 8:20 (NIV)

O LORD my God, in thee do I put my trust: save me from all them that persecute me, and deliver me.
Psalm 7:1

Blessed are you when people insult you, persecute you and falsely say all kinds of evil against you because of me. *Matthew 5:11* (NIV)

You have heard that it hath been said, Thou shalt love thy neighbor, and hate thine enemy. But I say unto you, Love your enemies, bless them that curse you, do good to them that hate you, and pray for them which despitefully use you, and persecute you . . . . *Matthew 5:43, 44*

Remember the word that I said unto you, the servant is not greater than his lord. If they have persecuted me, they will also persecute you; if they have kept my saying, they will keep yours also.

John 15:20

cults.

For many shall come in my name, saying, I am Christ; and shall deceive many. *Mark 13:6*

As we said before, so say I now again, if any man preach any other gospel unto you than that ye have received, let him be accursed. *Galatians 1:9*

For the time will come when men will not put up with sound doctrine. Instead, to suit their own desires, they will gather around them a great number of teachers to say what their itching ears want to hear. They will turn their ears away from the truth and turn aside to myths.
2 Timothy 4:3, 4 (NIV)

For I testify unto every man that heareth the words of the prophecy of this book, If any man shall add unto these things, God shall add unto him the plagues that are written in this book: And if any man shall take away from the words of the book of this prophecy, God shall take away his part out

of the book of life, and out of the holy city, and from the things which are written in this book.
Revelation 22:18, 19

For no one can lay any foundation other than the one already laid, which is Jesus Christ.
1 Corinthians 3:11 (NIV)

Who is a liar but he that denieth that Jesus is the Christ? He is antichrist, that denieth the Father and the Son.   *1 John 2:22*

Neither is there salvation in any other: for there is none other name under heaven given among men, whereby we must be saved.   *Acts 4:12*

See to it that no one takes you captive through hollow and deceptive philosophy, which depends on human tradition and the basic principles of this world rather than on Christ.   *Colossians 2:8* (NIV)

Then if any man shall say unto you, Lo, here is Christ, or there; believe it not. For there shall arise false Christs, and false prophets and shall shew great signs and wonders; insomuch that, if it were possible, they shall deceive the very elect. Behold, I have told you before. Wherefore if they shall say unto you, Behold, he is in the desert; go not forth: behold, he is in the secret chambers; believe it not.
Matthew 24:23-26

But evil men and seducers shall wax worse and worse, deceiving, and being deceived. But continue thou in the things which thou hast learned and hast been assured of, knowing of whom thou hast learned them . . . .   *2 Timothy 3:13, 14*

For such are false apostles, deceitful workers, transforming themselves into the apostles of Christ. And no marvel; for Satan himself is transformed into an angel of light.   *2 Corinthians 11:13, 14*

. . . For this purpose the Son of God was manifested, that he might destroy the works of the devil.
1 John 3:8

DANCING.

To every thing there is a season, and a time to every purpose under the heaven ... A time to weep, and a time to laugh; a time to mourn, and a time to dance .... *Ecclesiastes 3:4*

And David danced before the LORD with all his might .... *2 Samuel 6:14*

Let them praise his name in the dance: let them sing praises unto him with the timbrel and harp.
Psalm 149:3

Then shall the virgin rejoice in the dance, both young men and old together: for I will turn their mourning into joy, and will comfort them, and make them rejoice from their sorrow.
Jeremiah 31:13

And Miriam the prophetess, the sister of Aaron, took a timbrel in her hand; and all the women went out after her with timbrels and with dances.
Exodus 15:20

Thou hast turned for me my mourning into dancing: thou hast put off my sackcloth, and girded me with gladness; to the end that my glory may sing praise to thee, and not be silent. O LORD my God, I will give thanks unto thee for ever.

Psalm 30:11, 12

dating.

No verses in the Bible specifically refer to dating. In Bible times, young men and women did not date. Their marriages were arranged by their parents.

Nevertheless, the Scripture gives many principles and promises that pertain to the practice of dating.

Do not be misled: "Bad company corrupts good character."   *1 Corinthians 15:33* (NIV)

The integrity of the upright shall guide them: but the perverseness of transgressors shall destroy them.
Proverbs 11:3

Do not be yoked together with unbelievers. For what do righteousness and wickedness have in common? Or what fellowship can light have with darkness?   *2 Corinthians 6:14*

Honour thy father and thy mother: that thy days may be long upon the land which the LORD thy God giveth thee.   *Exodus 20:12*

ARMED AND DANGEROUS 73

Even a child is known by his doings, whether his work be pure, whether it be right. *Proverbs 20:11*

I therefore ... beseech you that ye walk worthy of the vocation wherewith ye are called ....
Ephesians 4:1

But take heed lest by any means this liberty of yours become a stumblingblock to them that are weak ... And through thy knowledge shall the weak brother perish, for whom Christ died? But when ye sin so against the brethren, and wound their weak conscience, ye sin against Christ.
1 Corinthians 8:9, 11, 12

Blessed are the pure in heart: for they shall see God. *Matthew 5:3*

And walk in love, as Christ also hath loved us, and hath given himself for us an offering and a sacrifice to God for a sweetsmelling savour. But fornication, and all uncleanness, or covetousness, let it not be once named among you, as becometh saints .... *Ephesians 5:2, 3*

How can a young man keep his way pure? By living according to your word ... I have hidden your word in my heart that I might not sin against you. *Psalm 119:9, 11* (NIV)

death.

Precious in the sight of the LORD is the death of his saints.   *Psalm 116:15*

Yea, though I walk through the valley of the shadow of death, I will fear no evil: for thou art with me; thy rod and thy staff they comfort me.
Psalm 23:4

In a moment shall they die, and the people shall be troubled at midnight, and pass away: and the mighty shall be taken away without hand.
Job 34:20

Wherefore, as by one man sin entered into the world, and death by sin; and so death passed upon all men, for that all have sinned . . . .
Romans 5:12

For the wages of sin is death; but the gift of God is eternal life through Jesus Christ our Lord.
Romans 6:23

For since by man came death, by man came also the resurrection of the dead. For as in Adam all die, even so in Christ shall all be made alive.
1 Corinthians 15:21, 22

Jesus said unto her, I am the resurrection, and the life: he that believeth in me, though he were dead, yet shall he live: And whosoever liveth and believeth in me shall never die. Believest thou this?
John 11:25, 26

And as it is appointed unto men once to die, but after this the judgment: So Christ was once offered to bear the sins of many; and unto them that look for him shall he appear the second time without sin unto salvation.   *Hebrews 10:27, 28*

For if we believe that Jesus died and rose again, even so them also which sleep in Jesus will God bring with him.   *1 Thessalonians 4:14*

Beloved, now are we the sons of God, and it doth not yet appear what we shall be: but we know that, when he shall appear, we shall be like him; for we shall see him as he is.   *1 John 3:2*

The last enemy that shall be destroyed is death.
1 Corinthians 15:26

And death and hell were cast into the lake of fire. This is the second death.   *Revelation 20:14*

76   Death

And God shall wipe away all tears from their eyes; and there shall be no more death, neither sorrow, nor crying, neither shall there be any more pain: for the former things are passed away.

Revelation 21:4

O death, where is thy sting? O grave, where is thy victory? The sting of death is sin; and the strength of sin is the law. But thanks be to God, which giveth us the victory through our Lord Jesus Christ.   *1 Corinthians 15:55-57*

DECEIT.

The words of his mouth are wicked and deceitful; he has ceased to be wise and to do good.
Psalm 36:3 (NIV)

The heart is deceitful above all things, and desperately wicked: who can know it? I the LORD search the heart, I try the reins, even to give every man according to his ways, and according to the fruit of his doings. *Jeremiah 17:9, 10*

. . . Deceitful men shall not live out half their days; but I will trust in thee. *Psalm 55:23*

Faithful are the wounds of a friend; but the kisses of any enemy are deceitful. *Proverbs 27:6*

Favour is deceitful, and beauty is vain: but a woman that feareth the LORD, she shall be praised.
Proverbs 31:30

He shall redeem their soul from deceit and violence: and precious shall their blood be in his sight.
Psalm 72:14

. . . Neither was any deceit in his mouth.
Isaiah 53:9

" 'Do not steal. Do not lie. Do not deceive one another.' "   *Leviticus 19:11* (NIV)

Let no man deceive you with vain words: for because of these things cometh the wrath of God upon the children of disobedience.
Ephesians 5:6

For "Whoever would love life and see good days must keep his tongue from evil and his lips from deceitful speech."   *1 Peter 3:10* (NIV)

But exhort one another daily, while it is called To day; lest any of you be hardened through the deceitfulness of sin.   *Hebrews 3:13*

defeat.

For a just man falleth seven times, and riseth up again: but the wicked shall fall into mischief.
Proverbs 24:16

He brought me up also out of an horrible pit, out of the miry clay, and set my feet upon a rock, and established my goings. And he hath put a new song in my mouth, even praise unto our God: many shall see it, and fear, and shall trust in the LORD.
Psalm 40:3, 4

The very fact that you have lawsuits among you means you have been completely defeated already. Why not rather be wronged? Why not rather be cheated? Instead, you yourselves cheat and do wrong, and you do this to your brothers.
1 Corinthians 6:7, 8 (NIV)

Therefore we do not lose heart. Though outwardly we are wasting away, yet inwardly we are being renewed day by day. *2 Corinthians 4:16*

Defeat

And he said unto me, My grace is sufficient for thee: for my strength is made perfect in weakness. Most gladly therefore will I rather glory in my infirmities, that the power of Christ may rest upon me.   *2 Corinthians 12:9*

demons.

For we wrestle not against flesh and blood, but against principalities, against powers, against the rulers of the darkness of this world, against spiritual wickedness in high places. Wherefore take unto you the whole armour of God, that you may be able to withstand in the evil day, and having done all, to stand.   *Ephesians 6:12, 13*

Now the Spirit speaketh expressly, that in the latter times some shall depart from the faith, giving heed to seducing spirits, and doctrines of devils.
1 Timothy 4:1

Beloved, believe not every spirit, but try the spirits whether they are of God ... And every spirit that confesseth not that Jesus Christ is come in the flesh is not of God . . . .   *1 John 4:1, 3*

Neither give place to the devil.   *Ephesians 4:27*

Be self-controlled and alert. Your enemy the devil prowls around like a roaring lion looking for someone to devour. Resist him, standing firm in the faith . . . .   *1 Peter 5:8, 9*

Submit yourselves therefore to God. Resist the devil, and he will flee from you.   *James 4:7*

Jesus rebuked the demon, and it came out of the boy, and he was healed from that moment.
Matthew 17:18 (NIV)

. . . They brought unto him many that were possessed with devils: and he cast out the spirits with his word, and healed all that were sick.
Matthew 8:16

So the devils besought him, saying, If thou cast us out, suffer us to go away into the herd of swine. And he said unto them, Go. And when they were come out, they went into the herd of swine: and, behold, the whole herd of swine ran violently down a steep place into the sea, and perished in the waters.   *Matthew 8:31, 32*

Then he called his twelve disciples together, and gave them power and authority over all devils, and to cure diseases.   *Luke 9:1*

. . . The sacrifices of pagans are offered to demons, not to God, and I do not want you to be

participants with demons.
1 Corinthians 10:20 (NIV)

Thou believest that there is one God; thou doest well: the devils also believe and tremble.
James 2:19

DEPRESSION.

The Spirit of the Lord God is upon me, because the LORD hath anointed me to preach good tidings unto the meek; he hath sent me to bind up the brokenhearted, to proclaim liberty to the captives, and the opening of the prison to them that are bound... To appoint unto them that mourn in Zion, to give unto them beauty for ashes, the oil of joy for mourning, the garment of praise for the spirit of heaviness; that they might be called trees of righteousness, the planting of the LORD, that he might be glorified.   *Isaiah 61:1, 3*

... Greater is he that is in you, than he that is in the world.   *1 John 4:4*

Why art thou cast down, O my soul? and why art thou disquieted within me? hope thou in God: for I shall yet praise him, who is the health of my countenance, and my God.   *Psalm 42:11*

A man's spirit sustains him in sickness, but a crushed spirit who can bear?
Proverbs 18:14 (NIV)

And Jesus came and spake unto them, saying, All power is given unto me in heaven and in earth.
Matthew 28:18

Thou wilt keep him in perfect peace, whose mind is stayed on thee: because he trusteth in thee. *Isaiah 27:3*

... Whatsoever things are true, whatsoever things are honest, whatsoever things are just, whatsoever things are pure, whatsoever things are lovely, whatsoever things are of good report; if there be any virtue, and if there be any praise, think on these things. *Philippians 4:8*

He giveth power to the faint; and to them that have no might he increaseth strength. *Isaiah 40:29*

Surely he hath born our griefs, and carried our sorrows: yet we did esteem him stricken, smitten of God, and afflicted. But he was wounded for our transgressions, he was bruised for our iniquities: the chastisement of our peace was upon him; and with his stripes we are healed. *Isaiah 53:4, 5*

... For the joy of the LORD is your strength.
Nehemiah 8:10

Peace I leave with you, my peace I give unto you: not as the world giveth, give I unto you. Let not your heart be troubled, neither let it be afraid.
John 14:27

discouragement.

Behold, the LORD thy God hath set the land before thee: go up and possess it, as the LORD God of thy Fathers hath said unto thee; fear not, neither be discouraged.   *Deuteronomy 1:21*

I cried unto God with my voice, even unto God with my voice; and he gave ear unto me.
Psalm 77:1

But they that wait upon the LORD shall renew their strength; they shall mount up with wings as eagles; they shall run, and not be weary; and they shall walk and not faint.   *Isaiah 40:31*

Have not I commanded thee? Be strong and of a good courage; be not afraid, neither be thou dismayed: for the LORD thy God is with thee whithersoever thou goest.   *Joshua 1:9*

He healeth the broken in heart, and bindeth up their wounds.   *Psalm 147:3*

We are troubled on every side, yet not distressed; we are perplexed, but not in despair ... Knowing that he which raised up the Lord Jesus shall raise up us also by Jesus, and shall present us with you.
2 Corinthians 4:8, 14

A merry heart doeth good like medicine: but a broken spirit drieth the bones. *Proverbs 17:22*

... A broken and a contrite heart, O God, thou wilt not despise. *Psalm 51:17*

divorce.

... A man will leave his father and mother and be united to his wife, and they will become one flesh.   *Genesis 2:24* (NIV)

... She shall be his wife; he may not put her away all his days.   *Deuteronomy 22:19*

He saith unto them, Moses because of the hardness of your hearts suffered you to put away your wives: but from the beginning it was not so. And I say unto you, Whosoever shall put away his wife, except it be for fornication, and shall marry another, committeth adultery: and whoso marrieth her which is put away doth commit adultery.
Matthew 19:8, 9

"I hate divorce," says the LORD God of Israel, "and I hate a man's covering himself with violence as well as with his garment," says the LORD Almighty. So guard yourself in your spirit, and do not break faith.   *Malachi 2:16* (NIV)

It hath been said, Whosoever shall put away his wife, let him give her a writing of divorcement: But I say unto you, that whosoever shall put away his wife, saving for the cause of fornication, causeth her to commit adultery: and whosoever shall marry her that is divorced committeth adultery.
Matthew 5:31, 32

And he saith unto them, Whosoever shall put away his wife, and marry another, committeth adultery against her. And if a woman shall put away her husband, and be married to another, she committeth adultery.   *Mark 10:11, 12*

To the married I give this command (not I, but the Lord): A wife must not separate from her husband. But if she does, she must remain unmarried or else be reconciled to her husband. And a husband must not divorce his wife.
1 Corinthians 7:10, 11 (NIV)

DOUBT.

The fool hath said in his heart, There is no God.
Psalm 14:1

I hate double-minded men, but I love your law.
Psalm 119:113 (NIV)

A double minded man is unstable in all his ways.
James 1:8

. . . Stop doubting and believe.
John 20:27 (NIV)

Jesus saith unto him, Thomas, because thou hast seen me, thou hast believed: blessed are they that have not seen, and yet have believed. *John 20:29*

And he saith unto them, Why are ye fearful, O ye of little faith? Then he arose, and rebuked the winds and the sea; and there was a great calm.
Matthew 8:26

But without faith it is impossible to please him: for he that cometh to God must believe that he is, and that he is a rewarder of them that diligently seek him.   *Hebrews 11:6*

Your word, O LORD, is eternal; it stands firm in the heavens. Your faithfulness continues through all generations.   *Psalm 119:89, 90 (NIV)*

I will instruct thee and teach thee in the way which thou shalt go: I will guide thee with mine eye.   *Psalm 32:8*

If any of you lack wisdom, let him ask of God, that giveth to all men liberally, and upbraideth not; and it shall be given him. But let him ask in faith, nothing wavering. For he that wavereth is like a wave of the sea driven with the wind and tossed. For let not that man think that he shall receive any thing of the Lord.   *James 1:5-7*

Wherefore seeing we also are compassed about with so great a cloud of witnesses, let us lay aside every weight, and the sin which doth so easily beset us, and let us run with patience the race that is set before us. Looking unto Jesus the author and finisher of our faith . . . .   *Hebrews 12:1, 2*

drug abuse.

For God hath not given us the spirit of fear; but of power, and love, and of a sound mind.
2 Timothy 1:7

But every man is tempted, when he is drawn away of his own lust, and enticed. Then when lust hath conceived, it bringeth forth sin: and sin, when it is finished, bringeth forth death.   *James 1:14, 15*

The Spirit of the Lord is upon me, because he hath anointed me to preach the gospel to the poor; he hath sent me to heal the brokenhearted, to preach deliverance to the captives and recovering of sight to the blind, to set at liberty them that are bruised, to preach the acceptable year of the Lord . . . And he began to say unto them, This day is this scripture fulfilled in your ears . . . And they were all amazed, and spake among themselves, saying, What a word is this! for with authority and power he commandeth the unclean spirits, and they come out.
Luke 4:18, 19, 21, 36

For you have spent enough time in the past doing what pagans choose to do—living in debauchery, lust, drunkenness, orgies, carousing and detestable idolatry.   *1 Peter 4:3* (NIV)

And ye shall know the truth, and the truth shall make you free ... If the Son therefore shall make you free, ye shall be free indeed.   *John 8:32, 36*

There hath not temptation taken you but such as is common to man: but God is faithful, who will not suffer you to be tempted above that ye are able; but will with the temptation also make a way to escape, that ye may be able to bear it.
1 Corinthians 10:13

enemies.

Bless them that curse you, and pray for them which despitefully use you. And unto him that smiteth thee on the one cheek offer also the other; and him that taketh away thy cloke forbid not to take thy coat also.   *Luke 6:28, 29*

When a man's ways please the LORD, he maketh even his enemies to be at peace with him.
Proverbs 16:7

Do not repay anyone evil for evil. Be careful to do what is right in the eyes of everybody. If it is possible, as far as it depends on you, live at peace with everyone. Do not take revenge, my friends, but leave room for God's wrath, for it is written: "It is mine to avenge; I will repay," says the Lord.
Romans 12:17-19 (NIV)

Ye have heard that it hath been said, Thou shalt love thy neighbor, and hate thine enemy. But I say unto you, Love your enemies, bless them that curse you, do good to them that hate you, and pray for them which despitefully use you, and persecute you . . . .   *Matthew 5:43, 44*

Then came Peter to him, and said, Lord, how oft shall my brother sin against me, and I forgive him? till seven times? Jesus saith unto him, I say not unto thee, Until seven times: but, until seventy times seven.   *Matthew 18:21, 22*

Judge not, and ye shall not be judged: condemn not, and ye shall not be condemned: forgive and ye shall be forgiven . . . .   *Luke 6:37*

So that we may boldly say, The Lord is my helper, and I will not fear what man shall do unto me.
Hebrews 13:6

The Lord shall cause thine enemies that rise up against thee to be smitten before thy face: they shall come out against thee one way, and flee before thee seven ways.   *Deuteronomy 28:7*

Through God we shall do valiantly: for he it is that shall tread down our enemies.   *Psalm 60:12*

Let those who love the LORD hate evil, for he guards the lives of his faithful ones and delivers them from the hand of the wicked.
Psalm 97:10 (NIV)

ENVY.

A sound heart is the life of the flesh: but envy the rottenness of the bones.   *Proverbs 14:30*

For where envying and strife is, there is confusion and every evil work.   *James 3:16*

Envy thou not the oppressor, and choose none of his ways.   *Proverbs 3:31*

Let not thine heart envy sinners: but be thou in the fear of the LORD all the day long.
Proverbs 23:17

Then he said to them, "Watch out! Be on your guard against all kinds of greed; a man's life does not consist in the abundance of his possessions."
Luke 12:15 (NIV)

Let your conversation be without covetousness; and be content with such things as ye have: for he hath said, I will never leave thee, nor forsake thee.
Hebrews 13:5

Anger is cruel and fury overwhelming, but who can stand before jealousy?   *Proverbs 27:4* (NIV)

But among you there must not be even a hint of sexual immorality, or any kind of impurity, or of greed, because these are improper for God's holy people.   *Ephesians 5:3* (NIV)

I know what it is to be in need, and I know what it is to have plenty. I have learned the secret of being content in any and every situation, whether well fed or hungry, whether living in plenty or in want. I can do everything through him who gives me strength.   *Philippians 4:12, 13* (NIV)

faith.

Now faith is the substance of things hoped for, the evidence of things not seen. *Hebrews 11:1*

But without faith it is impossible to please him: for he that cometh to God must believe that he is, and that he is a rewarder of them that diligently seek him. *Hebrews 11:6*

So then faith cometh by hearing, and hearing by the word of God. *Romans 10:17*

For by grace are ye saved through faith; and that not of yourselves: it is the gift of God: Not of works, lest any man should boast. *Ephesians 2:8, 9*

. . . For whatsoever is not of faith is sin.
Romans 14:23

Therefore being justified by faith, we have peace with God through our Lord Jesus Christ.
Romans 5:1

And Jesus answering saith unto them, Have faith in God.   *Mark 11:22*

"... I tell you the truth, if you have faith as small as a mustard seed, you can say to this mountain, 'Move from here to there' and it will move. Nothing will be impossible for you . . . ."
Matthew 17:20 (NIV)

I am crucified with Christ: nevertheless I live; yet not I, but Christ liveth in me: and the life which I now live in the flesh I live by the faith of the Son of God, who loved me, and gave himself for me.
Galatians 2:20

Wherein ye greatly rejoice, though now for a season, if need be, ye are in heaviness through manifold temptations: That the trial of your faith, being much more precious than of gold that perisheth, though it be tried with fire, might be found unto praise and honour and glory at the appearing of Jesus Christ: Whom having not seen, ye love; in whom, though now ye see him not, yet believing, ye rejoice with joy unspeakable and full of glory: Receiving the end of your faith, even the salvation of your souls.   *1 Peter 1:6-9*

fame.

LORD, I have heard of your fame; I stand in awe of your deeds, O LORD. *Habakkuk 3:2 (NIV)*

So then neither is he that planteth any thing, neither he that watereth; but God that giveth the increase. Now he that planteth and he that watereth are one: and every man shall receive his own reward according to his own labour. *1 Corinthians 3:7, 8*

Let no man deceive himself. If any man among you seemeth to be wise in this world, let him become a fool, that he may be wise. For the wisdom of this world is foolishness with God. For it is written, He taketh the wise in their own craftiness. And again, The Lord knoweth the thoughts of the wise, that they are vain. Therefore let no man glory in men . . . . *1 Corinthians 3:18-21*

Thy name, O LORD, endureth for ever; and thy memorial, O LORD, throughout all generations.
Psalm 135:13

The memory of the just is blessed: but the name of the wicked shall rot.   *Proverbs 10:7*

A good name is rather to be chosen than great riches, and loving favour rather than silver and gold.   *Proverbs 22:1*

FEAR.

The Lord is my light and my salvation; whom shall I fear? the Lord is the strength of my life, of whom shall I be afraid? *Psalm 27:1*

But now thus saith the LORD that created thee ... Fear not: for I have redeemed thee, I have called thee by thy name; thou art mine. When thou passest through the waters, I will be with thee, and through the rivers they shall not overflow thee: when thou walkest through the fire, thou shalt not be burned; neither shall the flame kindle upon thee.
Isaiah 43:1, 2

I sought the Lord, and he heard me, and delivered me from all my fears. *Psalm 34:4*

Peace I leave with you, My peace I give unto you: not as the world giveth, give I unto you. Let not your heart be troubled, neither let it be afraid.
John 14:27

ARMED AND DANGEROUS 103

Fear thou not; for I am with thee: be not dismayed; for I am thy God: I will strengthen thee; yea, I will help thee; yea, I will uphold thee with the right hand of my righteousness. *Isaiah 41:10*

For God hath not given us the spirit of fear, but of power, and of love, and of a sound mind.
2 Timothy 1:7

Do not be anxious about anything, but in everything, by prayer and petition, with thanksgiving, present your requests to God. And the peace of God, which transcends all understanding, will guard your hearts and your minds in Christ Jesus.
Philippians 4:6, 7 (NIV)

... for he hath said, I will never leave thee, nor forsake thee ... The Lord is my helper, and I will not fear what man shall do unto me.
Hebrews 13:5, 6

flattery.

The LORD shall cut off all flattering lips, and the tongue that speaketh proud things . . . .
Psalm 12:3

A lying tongue hateth those that are afflicted by it; and a flattering mouth worketh ruin.
Proverbs 26:28

The transgression of the wicked saith within my heart, that there is no fear of God before his eyes. For he flattereth himself in his own eyes, until his iniquity be found to be hateful.   *Psalm 36:1, 2*

. . . Meddle not with him that flattereth with his lips.   *Proverbs 20:19*

For such people are not serving our Lord Christ, but their own appetites. By smooth talk and flattery they deceive the minds of naive people.
Romans 16:18 (NIV)

He that rebuketh a man afterwards shall find more favour than he that flattereth with the tongue.
Proverbs 28:23

A man that flattereth his neighbor spreadeth a net for his feet. *Proverbs 29:5*

These men are grumblers and faultfinders; they follow their own evil desires; they boast about themselves and flatter others for their own advantage. *Jude 16* (NIV)

For there shall be no more any vain vision nor flattering divination within the house of Israel.
Ezekiel 12:24

forgiveness.

Forgiveness from God:

Blessed is he whose transgressions are forgiven, whose sins are covered. Blessed is the man whose sin the LORD does not count against him and in whose spirit is no deceit.   *Psalm 32:1, 2* (NIV)

Have mercy upon me, O God, according to thy lovingkindness: according unto the multitude of thy tender mercies blot out my transgressions. Wash me thoroughly from mine iniquity, and cleanse me from my sin.   *Psalm 51:1, 2*

For I will be merciful to their unrighteousness, and their sins and their iniquities will I remember no more.   *Hebrews 8:12*

I, even I, am he that blotteth out thy transgressions for mine own sake, and will not remember thy sins.   *Isaiah 43:25*

Let the wicked forsake his way, and the unrighteous man his thoughts: and let him return unto the LORD, and he will have mercy upon him; and to our God, for he will abundantly pardon.   *Isaiah 55:7*

He that covereth his sins shall not prosper: but whoso confesseth and forsaketh them shall have mercy.   *Proverbs 28:13*

If we say that we have no sin, we deceive ourselves, and the truth is not in us. If we confess our sins, he is faithful and just to forgive us our sins, and to cleanse us from all unrighteousness.
1 John 1:8, 9

Praise the LORD, O my soul, and forget not all his benefits—who forgives all your sins and heals all your diseases, who redeems your life from the pit and crowns you with love and compassion, who satisfies your desires with good things so that your youth is renewed like the eagle's.
Psalm 103:2-5 (NIV)

Forgiveness of Each Other:

Blessed are the merciful: for they shall obtain mercy.   *Matthew 5:7*

And when ye stand praying, forgive, if ye have ought against any: that your Father also which is in heaven may forgive you your trespasses. But if

ye do not forgive, neither will your Father which is in heaven forgive your trespasses.
Mark 11:25, 26

But love ye your enemies, and do good, and lend, hoping for nothing again; and your reward shall be great, and ye shall be the children of the Highest: for he is kind unto the unthankful and to the evil.
Luke 6:35

If thine enemy be hungry, give him bread to eat; and if he be thirsty, give him water to drink: For thou shalt heap coals of fire upon his head, and the LORD shall reward thee. *Proverbs 25:21, 22*

And be ye kind one to another, tenderhearted, forgiving one another, even as God for Christ's sake hath forgiven you. *Ephesians 4:32*

Take heed to yourselves: If thy brother trespass against thee, rebuke him; and if he repent, forgive him. And if he trespass against thee seven times in a day, and seven times in a day turn again to thee, saying, I repent; thou shalt forgive him.
Luke 17:3, 4

Then came Peter to him, and said, Lord, how oft shall my brother sin against me, and I forgive him? till seven times? Jesus saith unto him, I say not unto thee, Until seven times: but, until seventy times seven. *Matthew 18:21, 22*

FRIENDS.

A friend loveth at all times.... *Proverbs 17:17*

Can two walk together, except they be agreed? *Amos 3:3*

A man that hath friends must shew himself friendly: and there is a friend that sticketh closer than a brother. *Proverbs 18:24*

Bear ye one another's burdens, and so fulfil the law of Christ. *Galatians 6:2*

Faithful are the wounds of a friend; but the kisses of an enemy are deceitful. *Proverbs 27:6*

He who covers over an offense promotes love, but whoever repeats the matter separates close friends. *Proverbs 17:9* (NIV)

If one falls down, his friend can help him up. But pity the man who falls and has no one to help him up! *Ecclesiastes 4:10* (NIV)

Friends

Rejoice with them that do rejoice, and weep with them that weep.   *Romans 12:15*

... Know ye not that the friendship of the world is enmity with God? Whosoever therefore will be a friend of the world is the enemy of God.
James 4:4

He that walketh with wise men shall be wise: but a companion of fools shall be destroyed.
Proverbs 13:20

Do not forsake your friend and the friend of your father, and do not go to your brother's house when disaster strikes you—better a neighbor nearby than a brother far away.   *Proverbs 27:10* (NIV)

Finally, be ye all of one mind, having compassion one of another, love as brethren, be pitiful, be courteous: Not rendering evil for evil, or railing for railing: but contrariwise blessing; knowing that ye are thereunto called, that ye should inherit a blessing.   *1 Peter 3:8, 9*

the future.

My son, forget not my law; but let thine heart keep my commandments: For length of days, and long life, and peace, shall they add to thee.
Proverbs 3:1, 2

And the world passeth away, and the lust thereof: but he that doeth the will of God abideth forever.
1 John 2:17

A man's heart deviseth his way: but the LORD directeth his steps. *Proverbs 16:9*

Commit thy works unto the LORD, and thy thoughts shall be established. *Proverbs 16:3*

Jesus said unto him, If thou canst believe, all things are possible to him that believeth. *Mark 9:23*

Without counsel purposes are disappointed: but in the multitude of counsellors they are established.
Proverbs 15:22

"For I know the plans I have for you," declares the LORD, "plans to prosper you and not to harm you, plans to give you hope and a future."
Jeremiah 29:11 (NIV)

Do not let your heart envy sinners, but always be zealous for the fear of the LORD. There is surely a future hope for you, and your hope will not be cut off. *Proverbs 23:17, 18* (NIV)

In my Father's house are many mansions: if it were not so, I would have told you. I go to prepare a place for you. And if I go and prepare a place for you, I will come again, and receive you unto myself; that where I am, there ye may be also.
John 14:2, 3

gambling.

In the sweat of thy face shalt thou eat bread, till thou return unto the ground . . . .   *Genesis 3:19*

. . . If any would not work, neither should he eat.
2 Thessalonians 3:10

. . . For the children ought not to lay up for the parents, but the parents for the children.
2 Corinthians 12:14

Whether therefore ye eat, or drink or whatsoever ye do, do all to the glory of God.
1 Corinthians 10:31

All things are lawful unto me, but all things are not expedient: all things are lawful for me, but I will not be brought under the power of any.
1 Corinthians 6:12

Set your affection on things above, not on things on the earth . . . Mortify therefore your members which are upon the earth; fornication, uncleanness, inordinate affection, evil concupiscence, and covetousness, which is idolatry: For which things' sake the wrath of God cometh on the children of disobedience . . . .   *Colossians 3:5, 6*

I beseech you therefore, brethren, by the mercies of God, that ye present your bodies a living sacrifice, holy, acceptable unto God, which is your reasonable service.   *Romans 12:1*

Thou shalt not steal. Thou shalt not covet . . . any thing that is thy neighbor's.   *Exodus 20:15, 17*

GIFTS FROM GOD.

Jesus answered and said unto her, If thou knewest the gift of God, and who it is that saith to thee, Give me to drink; thou wouldest have asked of him, and he would have given thee living water. *John 4:10*

... The gift of God is eternal life through Jesus Christ our Lord. *Romans 6:23*

For by grace are ye saved through faith; and that not of yourselves: it is the gift of God ....
Ephesians 2:8

If ye then, being evil, know how to give good gifts unto your children: how much more shall your heavenly Father give the Holy Spirit to them that ask him? *Luke 11:13*

... Wait for the promise of the Father, which, saith he, ye have heard of me. *Acts 1:4*

Then Peter said unto them, Repent, and be baptized every one of you in the name of Jesus Christ for the remission of sins, and ye shall receive the gift of the Holy Ghost. For the promise is unto you, and to your children, and to all that are afar off, even as many as the Lord our God shall call.
Acts 2:38, 39

... But each man has his own gift from God; one has this gift, another has that.
1 Corinthians 7:7 (NIV)

We have different gifts, according to the grace given us .... *Romans 12:6*

Now there are diversities of gifts, but the same Spirit ... And there are diversities of operations, but it is the same God which worketh all in all. But the manifestation of the Spirit is given to every man to profit withal. *1 Corinthians 12:4, 6, 7*

And God hath set some in the church, first apostles, secondarily prophets, thirdly teachers, after that miracles, then gifts of healings, helps, governments, diversities of tongues. Are all apostles? are all prophets? are all teachers? are all workers of miracles? Have all the gifts of healings? do all speak with tongues? do all interpret? But covet earnestly the best gifts: and yet shew I unto you a more excellent way. *1 Corinthians 12:28-31*

. . . Since you are eager to have spiritual gifts, try to excel in gifts that build up the church.
1 Corinthians 14:12 (NIV)

Neglect not the gift that is in thee, which was given thee by prophecy, with the laying on of the hands of the presbytery. *1 Timothy 4:14*

. . . Stir up the gift of God, which is in thee . . . .
2 Timothy 1:6

Every good gift and every perfect gift is from above, and cometh down from the Father of lights, with whom is no variableness, neither shadow of turning. *James 1:17*

Each one should use whatever gift he has received to serve others, faithfully administering God's grace in its various forms. *1 Peter 4:10* (NIV)

giving.

Give and it shall be given unto you; good measure, pressed down, and shaken together, and running over, shall men give unto your bosom. For with the same measure that ye mete withal it shall be measured to you again. *Luke 6:38*

... The righteous giveth and spareth not.
Proverbs 21:26

... Freely ye have received, freely give.
Matthew 10:8

One man gives freely, yet gains even more; another withholds unduly, but comes to poverty.
Proverbs 11:24 (NIV)

... Remember the words of the Lord Jesus, how he said, It is more blessed to give than to receive.
Acts 20:35

Will a man rob God? Yet ye have robbed me. But ye say, Wherein have we robbed thee? In tithes and offerings ... Bring ye all the tithes into the storehouse, that there may be meat in mine house, and prove me now herewith, saith the LORD of hosts, if I will not open you the windows of heaven, and pour you out a blessing, that there shall not be room enough to receive it. And I will rebuke the devourer for your sakes .... *Malachi 3:8, 10, 11*

"And if anyone gives even a cup of cold water to one of these little ones because he is my disciple, I tell you the truth, he will certainly not lose his reward." *Matthew 10:42* (NIV)

Every man according as he purposeth in his heart, so let him give; not grudgingly, or of necessity: for God loveth a cheerful giver. *2 Corinthians 9:7*

Honor the LORD with your wealth, with the firstfruits of all your crops; then your barns will be filled to overflowing, and your vats will brim over with new wine. *Proverbs 3:9, 10* (NIV)

A generous man will prosper; he who refreshes others will himself be refreshed.
Proverbs 11:25 (NIV)

goals.

Not as though I had already attained, either were already perfect... but this one thing I do, forgetting those things which are behind, and reaching forth unto those things which are before, I press toward the mark for the prize of the high calling of God in Christ Jesus.   *Philippians 3:12-14*

So we make it our goal to please him, whether we are at home in the body or away from it.
2 Corinthians 5:9 (NIV)

The goal of this command is love, which comes from a pure heart and a good conscience and a sincere faith.   *1 Timothy 1:5* (NIV)

Delight thyself also in the LORD, and he shall give thee the desires of thine heart. Commit thy way unto the LORD; trust also in him; and he shall bring it to pass.   *Psalm 37:4, 5*

Do you not know that in a race all the runners run, but only one gets the prize? Run in such a way

as to get the prize. Everyone who competes in the games goes into strict training. They do it to get a crown that will not last; but we do it to get a crown that will last forever.
1 Corinthians 9:24, 25 (NIV)

Wherefore seeing we also are compassed about with so great a cloud of witnesses, let us lay aside every weight, and the sin which doth so easily beset us, and let us run with patience the race that is set before us, looking unto Jesus the author and finisher of our faith; who for the joy that was set before him endured the cross, despising the shame, and is set down at the right hand of the throne of God.
Hebrews 12:1, 2

Let us not become weary in doing good, for at the proper time we will reap a harvest if we do not give up.   *Galatians 6:9* (NIV)

GOSSIP.

A gossip betrays a confidence; so avoid a man who talks too much.   *Proverbs 20:19* (NIV)

A talebearer revealeth secrets: but he that is of a faithful spirit concealeth the matter.
Proverbs 11:13

The words of a gossip are like choice morsels; they go down to a man's inmost parts.
Proverbs 18:8 (NIV)

"Do not go about spreading slander among your people ... I am the LORD." *Leviticus 19:16* (NIV)

Where no wood is, there the fire goeth out: so where there is no talebearer, the strife ceaseth. As coals are to burning coals, and wood to fire; so is a contentious man to kindle strife.   *Proverbs 26:20, 21*

I said, I will take heed to my ways, that I sin not with my tongue . . . .   *Psalm 39:1*

If any man among you seem to be religious, and bridleth not his tongue, but deceiveth his own heart, this man's religion is vain. *James 1:26*

These six things doth the LORD hate: yea, seven are an abomination unto him: a proud look, a lying tongue, and hands that shed innocent blood, an heart that deviseth wicked imaginations, feet that be swift in running to mischief, a false witness that speaketh lies, and he that soweth discord among brethren. *Proverbs 6:16-19*

Keep thy tongue from evil, and thy lips from speaking guile. *Psalm 34:13*

. . . The tongue is a little member, and boasteth great things. Behold, how great a matter a little fire kindleth! Out of the same mouth proceedeth blessing and cursing. My brethren, these things ought not so to be. *James 3:5, 10*

grief.

Blessed are they that mourn for they shall be comforted. *Matthew 5:4*

Jesus wept. Then said the Jews, Behold how he loved him! *John 11:35, 36*

Let not your heart be troubled: ye believe in God, believe also in me. *John 14:1*

Blessed be the God and Father of our Lord Jesus Christ, which according to his abundant mercy hath begotten us again unto a lively hope by the resurrection of Jesus Christ from the dead, to an inheritance incorruptible, and undefiled, and that fadeth not away, reserved in heaven for you, who are kept by the power of God through faith unto salvation ready to be revealed in the last time. *1 Peter 1:3-5*

For we know that if our earthly house of this tabernacle were dissolved, we have a building of God, an house not made with hands, eternal in heavens.
2 Corinthians 5:1

Brothers, we do not want you to be ignorant about those who fall asleep, or to grieve like the rest of men, who have no hope. We believe that Jesus died and rose again and so we believe that God will bring with Jesus those who have fallen asleep in him.
1 Thessalonians 4.13, 14 (NIV)

guilt.

For whosoever shall keep the whole law, and yet offend in one point, he is guilty of all. *James 2:10*

He that covereth his sins shall not prosper: but whoso confesseth and forsaketh them shall have mercy. *Proverbs 28:13*

When I kept silent, my bones wasted through my groaning all day long ... Then I acknowledged my sin to you and did not cover up my iniquity. I said, "I will confess my transgressions to the LORD"— and you forgave the guilt of my sin.
Psalm 32:3, 4 (NIV)

"Although you wash yourself with soda and use an abundance of soap, the stain of your guilt is still before me ..." declares the Sovereign LORD.
Jeremiah 2:22 (NIV)

Come now, and let us reason together saith the LORD: though your sins be as scarlet, they shall be as white as snow; though they be red like crimson, they shall be as wool.   *Isaiah 1:18*

As far as the east is from the west, so far hath he removed our transgressions from us.
Isaiah 1:18

My guilt has overwhelmed me like a burden too heavy to bear.   *Psalm 38:4* (NIV)

For the LORD your God is gracious and merciful, and will not turn away his face from you, if ye return unto him.   *2 Chronicles 30:9*

. . . Thine iniquity is taken away, and thy sin purged.   *Isaiah 6:7*

If we say that we have fellowship with him, and walk in darkness, we lie, and do not the truth: But if we walk in the light, as he is in the light, we have fellowship one with another, and the blood of Jesus Christ his Son cleanseth us from all sin.
1 John 1:6, 7

There is therefore now no condemnation to them which are in Christ Jesus, who walk not after the flesh, but after the Spirit.   *Romans 8:1*

Therefore, brothers, since we have confidence to enter the Most Holy Place by the blood of Jesus . . . let us draw near to God with a sincere heart in full assurance of faith, having our hearts sprinkled to cleanse us from a guilty conscience and having our bodies washed with pure water.

Hebrews 10:19, 22 (NIV)

HEALING.

Is any among you afflicted? let him pray ... Is any sick among you? let him call for the elders of the church; and let them pray over him, anointing him with oil in the name of the Lord: And the prayer of faith shall save the sick, and the Lord shall raise him up; and if he have committed sins, they shall be forgiven him. Confess your faults one to another, and pray one for another, that ye may be healed. The effectual fervent prayer of a righteous man availeth much.   *James 5:13-16*

He gives strength to the weary and increases the power of the weak ... those who hope in the Lord will renew their strength.   *Isaiah 40:29, 31* (NIV)

"But I will restore you to health and heal your wounds," declares the LORD ....
Jeremiah 30:17 (NIV)

Bless the LORD, O my soul: and all that is within me, bless his holy name ... Who forgiveth all thine

iniquities; who healeth all thy diseases . . . .
Psalm 103:1, 3

. . . If thou wilt diligently hearken to the voice of the LORD thy God, and wilt do that which is right in his sight, and wilt give ear to his commandments, and keep all his statutes, I will put none of these diseases upon thee, which I have brought upon the Egyptians: for I am the LORD that healeth thee.   *Exodus 15:26*

He healeth the broken in heart, and bindeth up their wounds.   *Psalm 147:3*

And Jesus went about all Galilee . . . healing all manner of sickness and all manner of disease among the people.   *Matthew 4:23*

And Jesus went about all the cities and villages, teaching in their synagogues, and preaching the gospel of the kingdom, and healing every sickness and every disease among the people.
Matthew 9:35

Then he called his twelve disciples together, and gave them power and authority over all devils, and to cure diseases. And he sent them to preach the kingdom of God, and to heal the sick.   *Luke 9:1, 2*

But he was wounded for our transgressions, he was bruised for our iniquities: the chastisement of our peace was upon him; and with his stripes we are healed.   *Isaiah 53:5*

Who his own self bare our sins in his own body on the tree, that we, being dead to sins, should live unto righteousness: by whose stripes ye were healed.
1 Peter 2:24

When Jesus saw him . . . and knew that he had been now a long time in that case, he saith unto him, wilt thou be made whole?   *John 5:6*

The apostles performed many miraculous signs and wonders among the people . . . Crowds gathered also from the towns around Jerusalem, bringing their sick and those tormented by evil spirits, and all of them were healed.   *Acts 5:12, 16* (NIV)

heaven.

You have come to Mount Zion, to the heavenly Jerusalem, the city of the living God. You have come to thousands upon thousands of angels in joyful assembly .... *Hebrews 12:22* (NIV)

For Christ did not enter a man-made sanctuary that was only a copy of the true one; he entered heaven itself, now to appear for us in God's presence. *Hebrews 9:24* (NIV)

In my Father's house are many mansions: if it were not so, I would have told you. I go to prepare a place for you. And if I go and prepare a place for you, I will come again, and receive you unto myself; that where I am, there ye may be also.
John 14:2, 3

But now they desire a better country, that is, an heavenly: Wherefore God is not ashamed to be called their God: for he hath prepared for them a city. *Hebrews 11:16*

Beloved, now are we the sons of God, and it doth not yet appear what we shall be: but we know that, when he shall appear, we shall be like him; for we shall see him as he is. *1 John 3:2*

... Eye hath not seen, nor ear heard, neither have entered the heart of man, the things which God hath prepared for them that love him.
1 Corinthians 2:9

Behold, I shew you a mystery; We shall not all sleep, but we shall all be changed, in a moment, in the twinkling of an eye, at the last trump: for the trumpet shall sound, and the dead shall be raised incorruptible, and we shall be changed.
1 Corinthians 15:51, 52

And I say unto you, that many shall come from the east and west, and shall sit down with Abraham, and Isaac, and Jacob, in the kingdom of heaven.
Matthew 8:11

After this I beheld, and, lo, a great multitude, which no man could number, of all nations, and kindreds, and people, and tongues, stood before the throne, and before the Lamb, clothed in white robes, and palms in their hands. *Revelation 7:9*

And they sing the song of Moses the servant of God, and the song of the Lamb, saying, Great and marvellous are thy works, Lord God Almighty; just

and true are thy ways, thou King of saints.
Revelation 15:3

And God shall wipe away all tears from their eyes; and there shall be no more death, neither sorrow, nor crying, neither shall there be any more pain: for the former things are passed away.
Revelation 21:4

And I saw no temple therein: for the Lord God Almighty and the Lamb are the temple of it. And the city had no need of the sun, neither of the moon, to shine in it: for the glory of God did lighten it, and the Lamb is the light thereof. And the nations of them which are saved shall walk in the light of it . . . . *Revelation 21:22-24*

hell.

The wicked shall be turned into hell, and all the nations that forget God.   *Psalm 9:17*

Stolen waters are sweet, and bread eaten in secret is pleasant. But he knoweth not that the dead are there; and that her guests are in the depths of hell.
Proverbs 9:17, 18

... God spared not the angels that sinned, but cast them down to hell, and delivered them into chains of darkness to be reserved for judgment ....
2 Peter 2:4

Enter ye in at the strait gate: for wide is the gate, and broad is the way, that leadeth to destruction, and many there be which go in thereat ....
Matthew 7:13

Ye have heard that it was said by them of old time, Thou shalt not kill; and whosoever shall kill shall be in danger of the judgment: But I say unto you,

136 Hell

That whosoever is angry with his brother without a cause shall be in danger of the judgment and whosoever shall say to his brother, Raca, shall be in danger of the council: but whosoever shall say, Thou fool, shall be in danger of hell fire.
Matthew 5:21, 22

How shall we escape, if we neglect so great salvation . . . .   *Hebrews 2:3*

And if thy hand offend thee, cut it off: it is better for thee to enter into life maimed, than having two hands to go into hell, into the fire that never shall be quenched: Where their worm dieth not, and the fire is not quenched.   *Mark 9:43, 44*

And besides all this, between us and you there is a great gulf fixed: so that they which would pass from hence to you cannot; neither can they pass to us, that would come from thence.   *Luke 16:26*

And I say unto you my friends, Be not afraid of them that kill the body, and after that have no more that they can do. But I will forewarn you whom ye shall fear: Fear him, which after he hath killed hath power to cast into hell; yea, I say unto you, Fear him.   *Luke 12:4, 5*

And the beast was taken, and with him the false prophet that wrought miracles before him, with which he deceived them that had received the mark of the beast, and them that worshipped his image. These both were cast alive into a lake of fire burning with brimstone.   *Revelation 19:20*

He will punish those who do not know God and do not obey the gospel of our Lord Jesus. They will be punished with everlasting destruction and shut off from the presence of the Lord and from the majesty of his power . . . .
2 Thessalonians 1:8, 9 (NIV)

And earth and hell were cast into the lake of fire. This is the second death. And whosoever was not found written in the book of life was cast into the lake of fire.   *Revelation 20:14, 15*

He that overcometh shall inherit all things; and I will be his God, and he shall be my son. But the fearful, and the unbelieving, and the abominable; and murderers, and whoremongers, and sorcerers, and idolaters, and all liars, shall have their part in the lake which burneth with fire and brimstone: which is the second death.   *Revelation 21:7, 8*

HOME.

These commandments that I give you today are to be upon your hearts. Impress them on your children. Talk about them when you sit at home and when you walk along the road, when you lie down and when you get up.   *Deuteronomy 6:6, 7* (NIV)

For I know him, that he will command his children and his household after him, and they shall keep the way of the Lord, to do justice and judgment . . . .   *Genesis 18:19*

Train up a child in the way he should go: and when he is old, he will not depart from it.
Proverbs 22:6

. . . Choose you this day whom ye will serve; but as for me and my house, we will serve the Lord.
Joshua 24:14, 15

I will behave myself wisely in a perfect way. O when wilt thou come unto me? I will walk within my house with a perfect heart.   *Psalm 101:2*

... If a widow has children or grandchildren, these should learn first of all to put their religion into practice by caring for their own family and so repaying their parents and grandparents, for this is pleasing to God.   *1 Timothy 5:4* (NIV)

Be careful to obey all these regulations I am giving you, so that it may always go well with you and your children after you, because you will be doing what is good and right in the eyes of the LORD your God.   *Deuteronomy 12:28* (NIV)

Better is a dry morsel, and quietness therewith, than an house full of sacrifices with strife.
Proverbs 17:1

Children, obey your parents in the Lord: for this is right. Honour thy father and mother; which is the first commandment with promise; that it may be well with thee, and thou mayest live long on the earth. And, ye fathers, provoke not your children to wrath: but bring them up in the nurture and admonition of the Lord.   *Ephesians 6:1-4*

homosexuality.

Do you not know that the wicked will not inherit the kingdom of God? Do not be deceived: Neither the sexually immoral nor idolaters nor male prostitutes nor homosexual offenders nor thieves nor the greedy nor drunkards nor slanderers nor swindlers will inherit the kingdom of God.
1 Corinthians 6:9, 10 (NIV)

Thou shalt not lie with mankind, as with womankind: it is abomination. *Leviticus 18:22*

If a man lies with a man as one lies with a woman, both of them have done what is detestable. They must be put to death; their blood will be on their own heads. *Leviticus 20:13* (NIV)

Wherefore God also gave them up to uncleanness through the lusts of their own hearts, to dishonour their own bodies between themselves: Who changed the truth of God into a lie, and worshipped and served the creature more than the Creator, who is blessed for ever. Amen. For this cause God gave them up unto vile affections: for even their women did change the natural use into that which is against nature: And likewise also the men, leaving the natural use of the woman, burned in their lust one toward another; men with men working that which is unseemly, and receiving in themselves that recompence of their error ... Who knowing the judgment of God, that they which commit such things are worthy of death, not only do the same, but have pleasure in them that do them. *Romans 1:24-27, 32*

And that is what some of you were. But you were washed, you were sanctified, you were justified in the name of the Lord Jesus Christ and by the Spirit of our God. *1 Corinthians 6:11* (NIV)

honesty.

Now the parable is this: the seed is the word of God... But that on the good ground are they, which in an honest and good heart, having heard the word, keep it, and bring forth fruit with patience.
Luke 8:11, 15

Thou knowest the commandments, Do not commit adultery, Do not kill, Do not steal, Do not bear false witness, Defraud not, Honour thy father and mother.   *Mark 10:19*

Do not use dishonest standards when measuring length, weight or quantity. Use honest scales and honest weights, an honest ephah and an honest hin. I am the LORD your God, who brought you out of Egypt.   *Leviticus 19:35, 36* (NIV)

... That no man should blame us in this abundance which is administered by us: providing for honest things, not only in the sight of the Lord, but also in the sight of men   *2 Corinthians 8:20, 21*

Thou shalt not have in thine house divers measures, a great and a small. But thou shalt have a perfect and just weight, a perfect and just measure shalt thou have: that thy days may be lengthened in the land which the LORD thy God giveth thee. For all that do such things, and all that do unrighteously, are an abomination unto the LORD thy God.
Deuteronomy 25:14-16

Who shall ascend into the hill of the LORD? or who shall stand in his holy place? He that hath clean hands, and a pure heart; who hath not lifted up his soul unto vanity, nor sworn deceitfully.
Psalm 24:3, 4

A truthful witness gives honest testimony, but a false witness tells lies.   *Proverbs 12:17* (NIV)

And herein do I exercise myself, to have always a conscience void of offence toward God, and toward men.   *Acts 24:16*

Pray for us: for we trust we have a good conscience, in all things willing to live honestly.
Hebrews 13:18

Better is a little with righteousness than great revenues without right.   *Proverbs 16:8*

HUMILITY.

Let this mind be in you, which was also in Christ Jesus: Who, being in the form of God, thought it not robbery to be equal with God: But made himself of no reputation, and took upon him the form of a servant, and was made in the likeness of men: And being found in fashion as a man, he humbled himself, and became obedient unto death, even the death of the cross.   *Philippians 2:5-8*

If my people, which are called by my name, shall humble themselves, and pray, and seek my face, and turn from their wicked ways; then will I hear from heaven, and will forgive their sin, and will heal their land.   *2 Chronicles 7:14*

He mocks proud mockers but gives grace to the humble.   *Proverbs 3:34* (NIV)

The fear of the LORD is the instruction of wisdom; and before honor is humility.   *Proverbs 15:33*

By humility and the fear of the LORD are riches, and honour, and life.   *Proverbs 22:4*

Now Moses was a very humble man, more humble than anyone else on the face of the earth.
Numbers 12:3 (NIV)

. . . For every one that exalteth himself shall be abased; and he that humbleth himself shall be exalted.
Luke 18:14

Whosoever therefore shall humble himself as this little child, the same is greatest in the kingdom of heaven.   *Matthew 18:4*

. . God resisteth the proud, but giveth grace to the humble.   *James 4:6*

Humble yourselves, therefore, under God's mighty hand, that he may lift you up in due time.
1 Peter 5:6 (NIV)

hypocrisy.

... Their throat is an open sepulchre; they flatter with their tongue.   *Psalm 5:9*

Wherefore the LORD said, Forasmuch as this people draw near me with their mouth, and their lips do honor me, but have removed their heart far from me.   *Isaiah 29:13*

They profess that they know God; but in works they deny him, being abominable, and disobedient, and unto every good work reprobate.
Titus 1:16

"Why do you look at the speck of saw-dust in your brother's eye and pay no attention to the plank in your own eye? How can you say to your brother, 'Brother, let me take the speck out of your eye,' when you yourself fail to see the plank in your own eye? You hypocrite, first take the plank out of your eye, and then you will see clearly to remove the speck from your brother's eye."   *Luke 6:41, 42 (NIV)*

ARMED AND DANGEROUS 147

"Woe to you, teachers of the law and Pharisees, you hypocrites! You shut the kingdom of heaven in men's faces. You yourselves do not enter, nor will you let those enter who are trying to."
Matthew 23:13 (NIV)

Woe unto you, scribes and Pharisees, hypocrites! for ye devour widows' houses, and for a pretence make long prayers: therefore, ye shall receive the greater damnation. *Matthew 23:14*

Woe to you, teachers of the law and Pharisees, you hypocrites! You travel over land and sea to win a single convert, and when he becomes one, you make him twice as much a son of hell as you are.
Matthew 23:15 (NIV)

Woe unto you, scribes and Pharisees, hypocrites! for ye pay tithe of mint and anise and cummin, and have omitted the weightier matters of the law, judgment, mercy, and faith: these ought ye to have done, and not to leave the other undone. Ye blind guides, which strain at a gnat, and swallow a camel.
Matthew 23:23, 24

Woe to you, teachers of the law and Pharisees, you hypocrites! You clean the outside of the cup and dish, but inside they are full of greed and self-indulgence. Blind Pharisee! First clean the inside of the cup and dish, and then the outside also will be clean. *Matthew 23:25, 26* (NIV)

Hypocrisy

Woe unto you, scribes and Pharisees, hypocrites! for ye are like unto whited sepulchres, which indeed appear beautiful outward, but are within full of dead men's bones, and of all uncleanness. Even so ye also outwardly appear righteous unto men, but within ye are full of hypocrisy and iniquity.
Matthew 23:27, 28

LORD, who shall abide in thy tabernacle? who shall dwell in thy holy hill? He that walketh uprightly, and worketh righteousness, and speaketh the truth in his heart. *Psalm 15:1, 2*

incest.

" 'No one is to approach any close relative to have sexual relations. I am the LORD.

" 'Do not dishonor your father by having sexual relations with your mother. She is your mother; do not have relations with her.' "

Leviticus 18:6, 7 (NIV)

" 'Do not have sexual relations with your sister, either your father's daughter or your mother's daughter, whether she was born in the same home or elsewhere.

" 'Do not have sexual relations with your son's daughter or your daughter's daughter; that would dishonor you.

" 'Do not have sexual relations with the daughter of your father's wife, born to your father; she is your sister.

" 'Do not have sexual relations with your father's sister; She is your father's close relative.

" 'Do not have sexual relations with your mother's sister, because she is your mother's close relative.

" 'Do not dishonor your father's brother by

approaching his wife to have sexual relations; she is your aunt.

" 'Do not have sexual relations with your daughter-in-law. She is your son's wife; do not have relations with her.

" 'Do not have sexual relations with your brother's wife; that would dishonor your brother.

" 'Do not have sexual relations with both a woman and her daughter. Do not have sexual relations with either her son's daughter or her daughter's daughter; they are her close relatives. That is wickedness.

" 'Do not take your wife's sister as a rival wife and have sexual relations with her while your wife is living.' "   *Leviticus 18:9-18* (NIV)

For whosoever shall commit any of these abominations, even the souls that commit them shall be cut off from among their people.   *Leviticus 18:29*

For the Victim of Incest

When my father and my mother forsake me, then the LORD will take me up.   *Psalm 27:10*

Fear thou not; for I am with thee: be not dismayed; for I am thy God: I will strengthen thee; yea, I will help thee; yea, I will uphold thee with the right hand of my righteousness. Behold, all they that are incensed against thee shall be ashamed and confounded . . . For I the LORD thy God will hold thy right hand, saying unto thee, Fear not; I will help thee. *Isaiah 41:10, 11, 13*

Do not be anxious about anything, but in everything, by prayer and petition, with thanksgiving, present your requests to God. And the peace of God, which transcends all understanding, will guard your hearts and your minds in Christ Jesus.
Philippians 4:6, 7 (NIV)

LAZINESS.

Laziness brings on deep sleep, and the shiftless man goes hungry.   *Proverbs 19:15* (NIV)

He becometh poor that dealeth with a slack hand: but the hand of the diligent maketh rich. He that gathereth in summer is a wise son: but he that sleepeth in harvest is a son that causeth shame.
Proverbs 10:4, 5

And withal they learn to be idle, wandering about from house to house; and not only idle, but tattlers also and busybodies, speaking things which they ought not.   *1 Timothy 5:13*

If a man is lazy, the rafters sag; if his hands are idle, the house leaks. *Ecclesiastes 10:18* (NIV)

Go to the ant, thou sluggard; consider her ways, and be wise . . . How long wilt thou sleep, O sluggard? when wilt thou arise out of thy sleep?
Proverbs 6:6, 9

Poverty and shame shall be to him that refuseth instruction: but he that regardeth reproof shall be honoured.   *Proverbs 13:18*

A little sleep, a little slumber, a little folding of the hands to rest—and poverty will come on you like a bandit and scarcity like an armed man.
Proverbs 6:10, 11 (NIV)

He also that is slothful in his work is brother to him that is a great waster.   *Proverbs 18:9*

We do not want you to become lazy, but to imitate those who through faith and patience inherit what has been promised.   *Hebrews 6:12* (NIV)

loneliness.

A father to the fatherless, a defender of widows, is God in his holy dwelling. God sets the lonely in families . . . .   *Psalm 68:5, 6* (NIV)

And ye are complete in him, which is the head of all principality and power.   *Colossians 2:10*

God is our refuge and strength, a very present help in trouble. Therefore will not we fear, though the earth be removed and though the mountains be carried into the midst of the sea; though the waters thereof roar and be troubled, though the mountains shake with the swelling thereof.   *Psalm 46:1-3*

And, behold, I am with thee, and will keep thee in all places whither thou goest . . . for I will not leave thee, until I have done that which I have spoken to thee of.   *Genesis 28:15*

I will not leave you comfortless: I will come to you.   *John 14:18*

. . . I will never leave thee, nor forsake thee. So that we may boldly say, the Lord is my helper, and I will not fear what man shall do unto me.
Hebrews 13:5, 6

. . . Lo, I am with you alway, even unto the end of the world. Amen.   *Matthew 28:20*

love.

And we have known and believed the love that God hath to us. God is love; and he that dwelleth in love dwelleth in God, and God in him.   *1 John 4:16*

Herein is love, not that we loved God, but that he loved us, and sent his Son to be the propitiation for our sins.   *1 John 4:10*

For God so loved the world, that he gave his only begotten Son, that whosoever believeth in him should not perish, but have everlasting life.   *John 3:16*

But God, who is rich in mercy, for his great love wherewith he loved us, even when we were dead in sins, hath quickened us together with Christ, (by grace ye are saved;) and hath raised us up together, and made us sit together in heavenly places in Christ Jesus . . . .   *Ephesians 2:4-6*

We love him, because he first loved us.
1 John 4:19

Greater love has no one than this, that one lay down his life for his friends. *John 15:13* (NIV)

How great is the love the Father has lavished on us, that we should be called children of God! And that is what we are! The reason the world does not know us is that it did not know him. *1 John 3:1* (NIV)

Our Love for God

The LORD preserveth all them that love him: but all the wicked will he destroy. *Psalm 145:20*

I love them that love me; and those that seek me early shall find me. *Proverbs 8:17*

For the Father himself loveth you, because ye have loved me, and have believed that I came out from God. *John 16:27*

Know therefore that the LORD your God is God; he is the faithful God, keeping his covenant of love to a thousand generations of those who love him and keep his commands. *Deuteronomy 7:9* (NIV)

Our Love for Each Other

Love must be sincere. Hate what is evil; cling to what is good. Be devoted to one another in brotherly love. Honor one another above yourselves.
Romans 12:9, 10 (NIV)

Love

A new commandment I give unto you, That ye love one another; as I have loved you, that ye also love one another. By this shall all men know that ye are my disciples, if ye have love one to another.
John 13:34, 35

Beloved, let us love one another: for love is of God; and every one that loveth is born of God, and knoweth God. He that loveth not knoweth not God; for God is love.   *1 John 4:7, 8*

If anyone says, "I love God," yet hates his brother, he is a liar. For anyone who does not love his brother, whom he has seen, cannot love God, whom he has not seen.   *1 John 4:20 (NIV)*

Love is patient, love is kind. It does not envy, it does not boast, it is not proud. It is not rude, it is not self-seeking, it is not easily angered, it keeps no record of wrongs. Love does not delight in evil but rejoices with the truth. It always protects, always trusts, always hopes, always perseveres . . . Love never fails.   *1 Corinthians 13:4-8 (NIV)*

LOYALTY.

Then they would put their trust in God and would not forget his deeds but would keep his commands. They would not be like their forefathers—a stubborn and rebellious generation, whose hearts were not loyal to God, whose spirits were not faithful to him.   *Psalm 78:7, 8* (NIV)

Thou shalt have no other gods before me. Thou shalt not bow down thyself to them, nor serve them: for I the LORD thy God am a jealous God . . . .
Exodus 20:3, 5

If it be so, our God whom we serve is able to deliver us from the burning fiery furnace, and he will deliver us out of thine hand, O king. But if not, be it known unto thee, O king, that we will not serve thy gods, nor worship the golden image which thou hast set up.   *Daniel 3:17, 18*

And Ruth said, Entreat me not to leave thee, or to return from following after thee: for whither thou

goest, I will go; and where thou lodgest, I will lodge: thy people shall be my people, and thy God my god: Where thou diest, will I die, and there will I be buried: the LORD do so to me, and more also, if ought but death part thee and me.
Ruth 1:16, 17

O LORD, God of our fathers Abraham, Isaac and Israel, keep this desire in the hearts of your people forever, and keep their hearts loyal to you.
1 Chronicles 29:18 (NIV)

lust.

Ye have heard that it was said by them of old time, Thou shalt not commit adultery: but I say to you, That whosoever looketh on a woman to lust after her hath committed adultery with her already in his heart.   *Matthew 5:27, 28*

Flee also youthful lusts: but follow righteousness, faith, charity, peace, with them that call on the Lord out of a pure heart.   *2 Timothy 2:22*

Do not lust in your heart after her beauty or let her captivate you with her eyes ... Can a man scoop fire into his lap without his clothes being burned? Can a man walk on hot coals without his feet being scorched? So is he who sleeps with another man's wife; no one who touches her will go unpunished.
Proverbs 6:25, 27-29 (NIV)

From whence come wars and fightings among you? come they not hence, even of your lusts that war in your members? Ye lust, and have not: ye

kill, and desire to have, and cannot obtain: ye fight and war, yet ye have not, because ye ask not. Ye ask, and receive not, because ye ask amiss, that ye may consume it upon your lusts. Ye adulterers and adulteresses, know ye not that the friendship of the world is enmity with God? whosoever therefore will be a friend of the world is the enemy of God.
James 4:1-4

Love not the world, neither the things that are in the world. If any man love the world, the love of the Father is not in him. For all that is in the world, the lust of the flesh, and the lust of the eyes, and the pride of life, is not of the Father, but is of the world. And the world passeth away, and the lust thereof: but he that doeth the will of God abideth for ever.   *1 John 2:15-17*

As obedient children, do not conform to the evil desires you had when you lived in ignorance.
1 Peter 1:14 (NIV)

. . . Remember all the commands of the LORD, that you may obey them and not prostitute yourselves by going after the lusts of your own hearts and eyes.   *Numbers 15:39* (NIV)

This I say then, Walk in the Spirit, and ye shall not fulfil the lust of the flesh. For the flesh lusteth against the Spirit, and the Spirit against the flesh:

and these are contrary the one to the other: so that ye cannot do the things that ye would.
Galatians 5:16, 17

. . . that each of you should learn to control his own body in a way that is holy and honorable, not in passionate lust like the heathen, who do not know God . . *1 Thessalonians 4:4* (NIV)

marriage.

And the LORD God said, It is not good that the man should be alone; I will make him an help-meet for him . . . And Adam said, This is now bone of my bones, and flesh of my flesh: she shall be called Woman, because she was taken out of Man. Therefore shall a man leave his father and his mother, and shall cleave unto his wife and they shall be one flesh.   *Genesis 2:18, 23, 24*

Whoso findeth a wife findeth a good thing, and obtaineth favor of the LORD.   *Proverbs 18:22*

Be ye not unequally yoked together with unbelievers: for what fellowship hath righteousness with unrighteousness? and what communion hath light with darkness?   *2 Corinthians 6:14*

Submit to one another out of reverence for Christ. Wives, submit to your husbands as to the Lord.
Ephesians 5:21, 22 (NIV)

ARMED AND DANGEROUS 165

Husbands, in the same way be considerate as you live with your wives, and treat them with respect as the weaker partner and as heirs with you of the gracious gift of life, so that nothing will hinder your prayers.   *1 Peter 3:7* (NIV)

Husbands, love your wives, even as Christ also loved the church, and gave himself for it . . . .
Ephesians 5:25

However, each one of you also must love his wife as he loves himself, and the wife must respect her husband.   *Ephesians 5:33* (NIV)

Marriage is honourable in all, and the bed undefiled: but whoremongers and adulterers God will judge.
Hebrews 13:4

Let thy fountain be blessed: and rejoice with the wife of thy youth. Let her be as the loving hind and pleasant roe; let her breasts satisfy thee at all times; and be thou ravished always with her love.
Proverbs 5:18, 19

The husband should fulfill his marital duty to his wife, and likewise the wife to her husband. The wife's body does not belong to her alone but also to her husband. In the same way, the husband's body does not belong to him alone but also to his wife. Do not deprive each other except by mutual consent and for a time, so that you may devote yourselves to prayer. Then come together again so that Satan will not tempt you because of your lack of self-control.   *1 Corinthians 7:3-7* (NIV)

Live joyfully with the wife whom thou lovest all the days of the life of thy vanity, which he hath given thee under the sun . . . for that is thy portion in this life . . . .   *Ecclesiastes 9:9*

MIRACLES.

You are the God who performs miracles; you display your power among the peoples.
Psalm 77:14 (NIV)

Seek the LORD, and his strength: seek his face evermore. Remember his marvellous works that he hath done; his wonders, and the judgments of his mouth . . . . *Psalm 105:4, 5*

And in that same hour he cured many of their infirmities and plagues, and of evil spirits; and unto many that were blind he gave sight. Then Jesus answering said unto them, Go your way, and tell John what things ye have seen and heard; how that the blind see, the lame walk, the lepers are cleansed, the deaf hear, the dead are raised, to the poor the gospel is preached. *Luke 7:21, 22*

And he could there do no mighty work, save that he laid his hands upon a few sick folk, and healed them. And he marvelled because of their unbelief . . . *Mark 6:5, 6*

168   Miracles

Jesus answered them, I told you, and ye believed not: the works that I do in my Father's name, they bear witness of me.   *John 10:25*

But though he had done so many miracles before them, yet they believed not on him . . . .
John 12:37

"Do not believe me unless I do what my Father does. But if I do it, even though you do not believe me, believe the miracles, that you may know and understand that the Father is in me, and I in the Father."   *John 10:37, 38* (NIV)

And many of the people believed on him, and said, When Christ cometh, will he do more miracles than these which this man hath done?   *John 7:31*

"This is a wicked generation. It asks for a miraculous sign, but none will be given it except the sign of Jonah. For as Jonah was a sign to the Ninevites, so also will the Son of Man be to this generation."
Luke 11:29, 30 (NIV)

And many other signs truly did Jesus in the presence of his disciples, which are not written in this book: But these are written, that ye might believe that Jesus is the Christ, the Son of God; and that believing ye might have life through his name.
John 20:30, 31

Believe me that I am in the Father, and the Father in me: or else believe me for the very works' sake. Verily, verily, I say unto you, He that believeth on me, the works that I do shall he do also; and greater works that these shall he do; because I go unto my Father.   *John 14:11, 12*

Everyone was filled with awe, and many wonders and miraculous signs were done by the apostles.
Acts 2:43 (NIV)

For the Jews require a sign, and the Greeks seek after wisdom: But we preach Christ crucified, unto the Jews a stumbling block, and unto the Greeks foolishness; but unto them which are called, both Jews and Greeks, Christ the power of God, and the wisdom of God.   *1 Corinthians 1:22-24*

... How shall we escape if we ignore such a great salvation? This salvation, which was first announced by the Lord, was confirmed to us by those who heard him. God also testified to it by signs, wonders, and various miracles, and gifts of the Holy Spirit distributed according to his will.
Hebrews 2:3, 4 (NIV)

money.

Whoever loves money never has enough; whoever loves wealth is never satisfied with his income . . . . *Ecclesiastes 5:10* (NIV)

For the love of money is the root of all evil: which while some coveted after, they have erred from the faith, and pierced themselves through with many sorrows. *1 Timothy 6:10*

"No servant can serve two masters. Either he will hate the one and love the other, or he will be devoted to the one and despise the other. You cannot serve both God and Money." *Luke 16:13* (NIV)

A little that a righteous man hath is better than the riches of many wicked. *Psalm 37:16*

Charge them that are rich in this world, that they be not highminded, nor trust in uncertain riches, but in the living God, who giveth us richly all things to enjoy. *1 Timothy 6:17*

He that is faithful in that which is least is faithful also in much: and he that is unjust in the least is unjust also in much. If therefore ye have not been faithful in the unrighteous mammon, who will commit to your trust the true riches? *Luke 16:10, 11*

Ho, every one that thirsteth, come ye to the waters, and he that hath no money; come ye, buy, and eat; yea, come, buy wine and milk without money and without price. Wherefore do ye spend money for that which is not bread? and your labour for that which satisfieth not? hearken diligently unto me, and eat ye that which is good, and let your soul delight itself in fatness. *Isaiah 55:1, 2*

But my God shall supply all your need according to his riches in glory by Christ Jesus.
Philippians 4:19

Wealth gotten by vanity shall be diminished: but he that gathereth by labour shall increase.
Proverbs 13:11

Better is little with the fear of the LORD than great treasure and trouble therewith.
Proverbs 15:16

He that trusteth in his riches shall fall: but the righteous shall flourish as a branch.
Proverbs 11:28

Whoso mocketh the poor reproacheth his Maker: and he that is glad at calamities shall not be unpunished.   *Proverbs 17:5*

. . . I have learned, in whatsoever state I am, therewith to be content. I know both how to be abased, and I know how to abound: every where and in all things I am instructed both to be full and to be hungry, both to abound and to suffer need.
Philippians 4:11, 12

Keep your lives free from the love of money and be content with what you have, because God has said, "Never will I leave you; never will I forsake you."   *Hebrews 13:5* (NIV)

His lord said unto him, Well done, thou good and faithful servant: thou hast been faithful over a few things, I will make thee ruler over many things: enter thou into the joy of thy lord.   *Matthew 25:21*

music.

Hear this, you kings! Listen, you rulers! I will sing to the LORD, I will sing; I will make music to the LORD, the God of Israel. *Judges 5:3* (NIV)

Praise him with the sound of the trumpet: praise him with the psaltery and harp. Praise him with the timbrel and dance: praise him with the stringed instruments and organs. Praise him upon the loud cymbals: praise him upon the high sounding cymbals. Let every thing that hath breath praise the LORD. Praise ye the LORD. *Psalm 150:3-6*

And at the dedication of the wall of Jerusalem they sought the Levites ... to bring them to Jerusalem, to keep the dedication with gladness, both with thanksgivings, and with singing, with cymbals, psalteries, and with harps. *Nehemiah 12:27*

And now shall mine head be lifted up above mine enemies round about me: therefore will I offer in

Music

his tabernacle sacrifices of joy; I will sing, yea, I will sing praises unto the LORD. *Psalm 27:6*

Praise the LORD with harp: sing unto him with the psaltery and an instrument of ten strings. Sing unto him a new song; play skilfully with a loud noise. *Psalm 33:2, 3*

Let them praise his name in the dance: let them sing praises unto him with the timbrel and harp.
Psalm 149:3

Let the word of my mouth, and the meditation of my heart, be acceptable in thy sight, O LORD, my strength and my redeemer. *Psalm 19:14*

Make a joyful noise unto the LORD, all the earth: make a loud noise, and rejoice, and sing praise.
Psalm 98:4

Speak to one another with psalms, hymns and spiritual songs. Sing and make music in your heart to the Lord, always giving thanks to God the Father for everything, in the name of our Lord Jesus Christ. *Ephesians 5:19, 20* (NIV)

OBEDIENCE.

See, I am setting before you today a blessing and a curse—the blessing if you obey the commands of the LORD your God that I am giving you today; the curse if you disobey the commands of the LORD your God and turn from the way that I command you today by following other gods, which you have not known.
Deuteronomy 11:26-28 (NIV)

(For the weapons of our warfare are not carnal, but mighty through God to the pulling down of strong holds;) Casting down imaginations, and every high thing that exalteth itself against the knowledge of God, and bringing into captivity every thought to the obedience of Christ.
2 Corinthians 10:4, 5

Thou shalt obey the voice of the LORD thy God, and do his commandments and his statutes, which I command thee this day. *Deuteronomy 27:10*

Obedience

And Samuel said, Hath the LORD as great delight in burnt-offerings and sacrifices, as in obeying the voice of the LORD? Behold, to obey is better than sacrifice, and to hearken than the fat of rams.
1 Samuel 15:22

If you love me, keep my commandments. If a man love me he will keep my words: and my Father will love him, and we will come unto him, and make our abode with him.   *John 14:15, 23*

For this is the love of God, that we keep his commandments: and his commandments are not grievous.   *1 John 5:3*

And he went a little farther, and fell on his face, and prayed, saying, O my Father, if it be possible, let this cup pass from me: nevertheless not as I will, but as thou wilt.   *Matthew 26:39*

And being found in fashion as a man, he humbled himself, and became obedient unto death, even the death of the cross.   *Philippians 2:8*

And hereby we do know that we know him, if we keep his commandments. He that saith, I know him, and keepeth not his commandments, is a liar, and the truth is not in him.   *1 John 2:3, 4*

And why call ye me, Lord, Lord, and do not the things which I say?   *Luke 6:46*

Therefore to him that knoweth to do good, and doeth it not, to him it is sin.   *James 4:17*

If ye know these things, happy are ye if ye do them.   *John 13:17*

Be ye doers of the word, and not hearers only, deceiving your own selves.   *James 1:22*

Not every one that saith unto me, Lord, Lord, shall enter into the kingdom of heaven; but he that doeth the will of my Father which is in heaven.
Matthew 7:21

the occult.

Let no one be found among you who sacrifices his son or daughter in the fire, who practices divination or sorcery, interprets omens, engages in witchcraft, or casts spells, or who is a medium or spiritist or who consults the dead. Anyone who does these things is detestable to the LORD, and because of these detestable practices the LORD your God will drive out those nations before you.
Deuteronomy 18:10-12 (NIV)

Saul died because he was unfaithful to the LORD; he did not keep the word of the LORD and even consulted a medium for guidance, and did not inquire of the LORD. So the LORD put him to death and turned the kingdom over to David son of Jesse.
1 Chronicles 10:13, 14 (NIV)

But the cowardly, the unbelieving, the vile, the murderers, the sexually immoral, those who practice magic arts, the idolaters and all liars—their place will be in the fiery lake of burning sulfur. This is the second death.   *Revelation 21:8* (NIV)

And the soul that turneth after such as have familiar spirits, and after wizards, to go a whoring after them, I will even set my face against that soul, and will cut him off from among his people.
Leviticus 20:6

. . . Greater is he that is in you, than he that is in the world.   *1 John 4:4*

Therefore shall evil come upon thee; thou shalt not know from whence it riseth: and mischief shall fall upon thee; thou shalt not be able to put it off: and desolation shall come upon thee suddenly, which thou shalt not know. Stand now with thine enchantments, and with the multitude of thy sorceries, wherein thou hast laboured from thy youth . . . Thou art wearied in the multitude of thy counsels. Let now the astrologers, the stargazers, the monthly prognosticators, stand up, and save thee from these things that shall come upon thee. Behold, they shall be as stubble; the fire shall burn them; they shall not deliver themselves from the power of the flame . . . none shall save thee.
Isaiah 47:11-15

Giving thanks unto the Father, which hath made us meet to be partakers of the inheritance of the saints in light: who hath delivered us from the power of darkness, and hath translated us into the kingdom of his dear Son: In whom we have redemption through his blood, even the forgiveness of sins . . *Colossians 1:12-14*

parents.

" 'Each of you must respect his mother and father . . . . ' "   *Leviticus 19:3* (NIV)

Whoso curseth his father or his mother, his lamp shall be put out in obscure darkness.
Proverbs 20:20

He who robs his father and drives out his mother is a son who brings shame and disgrace.
Proverbs 19:26 (NIV)

Whoso robbeth his father or his mother, and saith, It is no transgression; the same is the companion of a destroyer.   *Proverbs 28:24*

The father of the righteous shall greatly rejoice: and he that begetteth a wise child shall have joy of him.   *Proverbs 23:24*

Parents

... Honor thy father and thy mother.   *Luke 18:20*

Children, obey your parents in all things: for this is well pleasing unto the Lord.   *Colossians 3:20*

Children, obey your parents in the Lord, for this is right. "Honor your father and mother"—which is the first commandment with a promise— "that it may go well with you and that you may enjoy long life on the earth."   *Ephesians 6:1-3* (NIV)

PATIENCE.

Rest in the LORD, and wait patiently for him: fret not thyself because of him who prospereth in his way, because of the man who bringeth wicked devices to pass. *Psalm 37:7*

... Be patient toward all men. See that none render evil for evil unto any man; but ever follow that which is good, both among yourselves, and to all men. *1 Thessalonians 5:14, 15*

But the fruit of the Spirit is love, joy, peace, patience . . . . *Galatians 5:22* (NIV)

... the patient in spirit is better than the proud in spirit. *Ecclesiastes 7:8*

... But we glory in tribulations also: knowing that tribulation worketh patience; and patience, experience; and experience, hope . . . .
Romans 5:3, 4

Patience

Love is patient, love is kind . . . it is not easily angered.   *1 Corinthians 13:3, 4* (NIV)

And let us not be weary in well doing: for in due season we shall reap, if we faint not.
Galatians 6:9

Be patient, then, brothers, until the Lord's coming. See how the farmer waits for the land to yield its valuable crop and how patient he is for the autumn and spring rains. You too, be patient and stand firm, because the Lord's coming is near.
James 5:7, 8 (NIV)

For ye have need of patience, that, after ye have done the will of God, ye might receive the promise.
Hebrews 10:36

peace.

Peace I leave with you, my peace I give unto you: not as the world giveth, give I unto you. Let not your heart be troubled, neither let it be afraid. *John 14:27*

Therefore being justified by faith, we have peace with God through our Lord Jesus Christ . . . .
Romans 5:1

And, having made peace through the blood of his cross, by him to reconcile all things unto himself; by him, I say, whether they be things in earth, or things in heaven. *Colossians 1:20*

Now the God of hope fill you with all joy and peace in believing, that ye may abound in hope, through the power of the Holy Ghost.
Romans 15:13

And the peace of God, which transcends all understanding, will guard your hearts and your minds in Christ Jesus. *Philippians 4:7* (NIV)

And we know that all things work together for good to them that love God, to them who are the called according to his purpose.   *Romans 8:28*

Depart from evil, and do good; seek peace, and pursue it.   *Psalm 34:14*

Follow peace with all men, and holiness, without which no man shall see the Lord . . . .
Hebrews 12:14

Thou wilt keep him in perfect peace, whose mind is stayed on thee: because he trusteth in thee
Isaiah 26:3

"I have told you these things, so that in me you may have peace. In this world you will have trouble. But take heart! I have overcome the world."
John 16:33 (NIV)

peer pressure.

Therefore, I urge you, brothers, in view of God's mercy, to offer your bodies as living sacrifices, holy and pleasing to God—this is your spiritual act of worship. Do not conform any longer to the pattern of this world, but be transformed by the renewing of your mind. Then you will be able to test and approve what God's will is—his good, pleasing and perfect will.   *Romans 12:1, 2* (NIV)

. . . Walk worthy of God, who hath called you unto his kingdom and glory.   *1 Thessalonians 2:12*

"Therefore come out from them and be separate, says the Lord. Touch no unclean thing, and I will receive you. I will be a Father to you, and you will be my sons and daughters, says the Lord Almighty."
2 Corinthians 6:17, 18 (NIV)

As obedient children, not fashioning yourselves according to the former lusts in your ignorance: But as he which hath called you is holy, so be ye holy in all manner of conversation; because it is written, Be ye holy; for I am holy. *1 Peter 1:14-16*

Since we have these promises, dear friends, let us purify ourselves from everything that contaminates body and spirit, perfecting holiness out of reverence for God. *2 Corinthians 7:1* (NIV)

Prove all things; hold fast that which is good. Abstain from all appearance of evil.
1 Thessalonians 5:21, 22

For God hath not called us unto uncleanness, but unto holiness. *1 Thessalonians 4:17*

But in your hearts set apart Christ as Lord. Always be prepared to give an answer to everyone who asks you to give the reason for the hope that you have. But do this with gentleness and respect, keeping a clear conscience, so that those who speak maliciously against your good behavior in Christ may be ashamed of their slander.
1 Peter 3:15, 16 (NIV)

PERSECUTION.

Blessed are those who are persecuted because of righteousness, for theirs is the kingdom of heaven. Blessed are you when people insult you, persecute you and falsely say all kinds of evil against you because of me. Rejoice and be glad, because great is your reward in heaven, for in the same way they persecuted the prophets who were before you.
Matthew 5:10-12 (NIV)

And ye shall be hated of all men for my name's sake: but he that endureth to the end shall be saved.
Matthew 10:22

All thy commandments are faithful: they persecute me wrongfully; help thou me.   *Psalm 119:86*

Remember the word that I said unto you, The servant is not greater than his lord. If they have persecuted me, they will also persecute you; if they have kept my saying, they will keep yours also.
John 15:20

Persecution

Bless them which persecute you: bless and curse not.   *Romans 12:14*

Yea, and all that will live godly in Christ Jesus shall suffer persecution.   *2 Timothy 3:12*

... When we are cursed, we bless; when we are persecuted, we endure it; when we are slandered, we answer kindly.   *1 Corinthians 4:12, 13* (NIV)

pornography.

Let this mind be in you, which was also in Christ Jesus . . . .   *2 Timothy 1:7*

Know ye not that the unrighteous shall not inherit the kingdom of God? Be not deceived: neither fornicators, nor idolaters, nor adulterers, nor effeminate, nor abusers of themselves with mankind, nor thieves, nor covetous, nor drunkards, nor revilers, nor extortioners shall inherit the kingdom of God.   *1 Corinthians 6:9, 10*

So I tell you this, and insist on it in the Lord, that you must no longer live as the Gentiles do, in the futility of their thinking. They are darkened in their understanding and separated from the life of God because of their ignorance that is in them due to the hardening of their hearts. Having lost all sensitivity, they have given themselves over to sensuality so as to indulge in every kind of impurity, with a continual lust for more. You, however, did not come to know Christ that way.   *Ephesians 4:17-20* (NIV)

And have no fellowship with the unfruitful works of darkness, but rather reprove them. For it is a shame even to speak of those things which are done of them in secret.   *Ephesians 5:11, 12*

Finally, brethren, whatsoever things are true, whatsoever things are honest, whatsoever things are just, whatsoever things are pure, whatsoever things are lovely, whatsoever things are of a good report; if there be any virtue, and if there be any praise, think on these things.   *Philippians 4:8*

prayer.

The eyes of the LORD are on the righteous and his ears are attentive to their cry; the righteous cry out, and the LORD hears them; he delivers them from all their troubles. The LORD is close to the brokenhearted and saves those who are crushed in spirit.   *Psalm 34:15, 17, 18* (NIV)

I will offer to thee the sacrifice of thanksgiving, and will call upon the name of the LORD.
Psalm 116:17

And when thou prayest, thou shalt not be as the hypocrites are: for they love to pray standing in the synagogues and in the corners of the streets, that they may be seen of men. Verily I say unto you, They have their reward. But thou, when thou prayest, enter into thy closet, and when thou hast shut thy door, pray to thy Father which is in secret: and thy Father which seeth in secret shall reward thee openly.   *Matthew 6:5, 6*

After this manner therefore pray ye: Our Father which art in heaven, Hallowed be thy name. Thy kingdom come. Thy will be done in earth, as it is in heaven. Give us this day our daily bread. And forgive us our debts, as we forgive our debtors. And lead us not into temptation, but deliver us from evil: For thine is the kingdom, and the power, and the glory, for ever. Amen.   *Matthew 6:9-13*

And all things, whatsoever ye shall ask in prayer, believing, ye shall receive.   *Matthew 21:22*

Ask, and it shall be given you; seek and ye shall find; knock, and it shall be opened unto you: For every one that asketh receiveth; and he that seeketh findeth; and to him that knocketh it shall be opened.
Matthew 7:7, 8

Therefore I say unto you, What things soever ye desire, when ye pray, believe that ye receive them, and ye shall have them. And when ye stand praying, forgive, if ye have ought against any: that your Father also which is in heaven may forgive you your trespasses.   *Mark 11:24, 25*

And whatsoever ye shall ask in my name, that will I do, that the Father may be glorified in the Son. If ye shall ask any thing in my name I will do it.   *John 14:24, 25*

If ye abide in me, and my words abide in you, ye shall ask what ye will, and it shall be done unto you. *John 15:7*

Is any among you afflicted? let him pray. Is any merry? let him sing psalms. Confess your faults one to another, and pray one for another, that ye may be healed. The effectual fervent prayer of a righteous man availeth much. *James 5:13, 16*

Pray without ceasing. *1 Thessalonians 5:17*

Praying always with all prayer and supplication in the Spirit, and watching thereunto with all perseverance and supplication for all saints . . . .
Ephesians 6:18

I exhort therefore, that, first of all, supplications, prayers, intercessions, and giving of thanks, be made for all men . . . . *1 Timothy 2:1*

Be careful for nothing; but in every thing by prayer and supplication with thanksgiving let your requests be made known unto God. *Philippians 4:6*

If I regard iniquity in my heart, the LORD will not hear me . . . . *Psalm 66:18*

The sacrifice of the wicked is an abomination to the LORD: but the prayer of the upright is his delight. *Proverbs 15:8*

PRIDE.

For all that is in the world, the lust of the flesh, and the lust of the eyes, and the pride of life, is not of the Father, but is of the world.   *1 John 2:16*

... God resisteth the proud, but giveth grace unto the humble.   *James 4:6*

For I say, through the grace given unto me, to every man that is among you, not to think of himself more highly than he ought to think....
Romans 12:3

When pride cometh, then cometh shame: but with the lowly is wisdom.   *Proverbs 11:2*

Every one that is proud in heart is an abomination to the LORD: though hand join in hand, he shall not be unpunished.   *Proverbs 16:6*

An high look, and a proud heart, and the plowing of the wicked, is sin.   *Proverbs 21:4*

Likewise ye younger, submit yourselves unto the elder. Yea, all of you be subject one to another, and be clothed with humility: for God resisteth the proud, and giveth grace to the humble.

1 Peter 5:5, 6

prophecy.

We have also a more sure word of prophecy; whereunto ye do well that ye take heed . . . Knowing this first, that no prophecy of the scripture is of any private interpretation. For the prophecy came not in old time by the will of man: but holy men of God spake as they were moved by the Holy Ghost.
2 Peter 1:19-21

. . . We which are alive and remain unto the coming of the Lord, shall not prevent them which are asleep. For the Lord himself shall descend from heaven with a shout, with the voice of the archangel, and with the trump of God: and the dead in Christ shall rise first . . . Then we which are alive and remain shall be caught up together with them in the clouds, to meet the Lord in the air: and so shall we ever be with the Lord. Wherefore comfort one another with these words. *1 Thessalonians 4:15-18*

I saw in the night visions, and, behold, one like the Son of man came with the clouds of heaven, and came to the Ancient of days, and they brought him near before him. And there was given him dominion, and glory, and a kingdom, that all people, nations, and languages, should serve him: his dominion is an everlasting dominion, which shall not pass away, and his kingdom that which shall not be destroyed.   *Daniel 7:13, 14*

Behold, he cometh with clouds; and every eye shall see him, and they also which pierced him: and all kindreds of the earth shall wail because of him. Even so, Amen.   *Revelation 1:7*

And then shall appear the sign of the Son of man in heaven: and then shall all the tribes of the earth mourn, and they shall see the Son of man coming in the clouds of heaven with power and great glory.
Matthew 24:30

Whosoever therefore shall be ashamed of me and of my words in this adulterous and sinful generation; of him also shall the Son of man be ashamed, when he cometh in the glory of his Father with holy angels.   *Mark 8:38*

But the day of the Lord will come as a thief in the night; in the which the heavens shall pass away with a great noise, and the elements shall melt with fervent heat, the earth also and the works that are therein shall be burned up. Seeing then that all these things shall be dissolved, what manner of persons ought ye to be in all holy conversation and godliness, looking for and hasting unto the coming of the day of God . . . Nevertheless we, according to his promise, look for new heavens and a new earth, wherein dwelleth righteousness . . . .

2 Peter 3:10-13

punishment.

"Your wickedness will punish you; your backsliding will rebuke you. Consider then and realize how evil and bitter it is for you when you forsake the LORD your God and have no awe of me," declares the Lord, the LORD Almighty.
Jeremiah 2:19 (NIV)

... The Lord Jesus shall be revealed from heaven with his mighty angels, in flaming fire taking vengeance on them that know not God, and that obey not the gospel of our Lord Jesus Christ.
1 Thessalonians 1:7, 8

For if the word spoken by angels was steadfast, and every transgression and disobedience received a just recompence of reward, how shall we escape, if we neglect so great salvation . . . .
Hebrews 2:2, 3

He that despised Moses' law died without mercy under two or three witnesses: Of how much sorer

punishment, suppose ye, shall he be thought worthy, who hath trodden under foot the Son of God, and hath counted the blood of the covenant, wherewith he was sanctified, an unholy thing, and hath done despite unto the Spirit of grace . . . It is a fearful thing to fall into the hands of the living God.
Hebrews 10:28, 29, 31

RESPECT.

Honour all men. Love the brotherhood. Fear God. Honour the king.   *1 Peter 2:17*

" 'Rise in the presence of the aged, show respect for the elderly and revere your God. I am the LORD.' "   *Leviticus 19:32* (NIV)

That all men should honour the Son, even as they honour the Father. He that honoureth not the Son honoureth not the Father which hath sent him.
John 5:23

But now the LORD declares . . . "Those who honor me I will honor, but those who despise me will be disdained."   *1 Samuel 2:30* (NIV)

. . . The wife must respect her husband.
Ephesians 5:33 (NIV)

Husbands, in the same way be considerate as you live with your wives, and treat them with respect as the weaker partner and as heirs with you of the gracious gift of life, so that nothing will hinder your prayers.   *1 Peter 3: 7* (NIV)

Honour thy father and thy mother: that thy days may be long upon the land which the LORD thy God giveth thee.   *Exodus 20:12*

restitution.

"A thief must certainly make restitution, but if he has nothing he must be sold to pay for his theft. If the stolen animal is found alive in his possession—whether ox or donkey or sheep—he must pay back double." *Exodus 22:3, 4* (NIV)

Men do not despise a thief, if he steal to satisfy his soul when he is hungry; but if he be found, he shall restore sevenfold; he shall give all the substance of his house. *Proverbs 6:30, 31*

"If anyone sins and is unfaithful to the LORD by deceiving his neighbor about something entrusted to him or left in his care or stolen, or if he cheats him . . . or whatever it was he swore falsely about; he must make restitution in full, add a fifth of the value to it and give it all to the owner."
Leviticus 6:2, 5 (NIV)

And Zacchaeus stood, and said unto the Lord; Behold, Lord, the half of my goods I give to the poor; and if I have taken any thing from any man by false accusation I restore him fourfold. And Jesus said unto him, This day is salvation come to this house . . . .   *Luke 19:8, 9*

resurrection.

O LORD, thou hast brought up my soul from the grave: thou hast kept me alive, that I should not go down to the pit. But thou, O Lord, be merciful unto me, and raise me up, that I may requite them.
Psalm 30:3; 41:10

And he saith unto them, Be not affrighted: Ye seek Jesus of Nazareth, which was crucified: he is risen; he is not here: behold the place where they laid him. But go your way, tell his disciples and Peter that he goeth before you into Galilee: there shall ye see him, as he said unto you.   *Mark 16:6, 7*

Christ died for our sins according to the scriptures; and that he was seen of Cephas, then of the twelve: after that, he was seen of above five hundred brethren at once: of whom the greater part remain unto this present, but some are fallen asleep. After that, he was seen of James; then of all the apostles. And last of all he was seen of me also . . . .
1 Corinthians 15:3-8

Resurrection

And if Christ be not risen, then is our preaching vain, and your faith is also vain ... And if Christ be not raised, your faith is vain; ye are yet in your sins ... If in this life only we have hope in Christ, we are of all men most miserable. But now is Christ risen from the dead, and become the firstfruits of them that slept.   *1 Corinthians 15:14, 17, 19, 20*

Jesus said unto her, I am the resurrection, and the life: he that believeth in me, though he were dead, yet shall he live: And whosoever liveth and believeth in me shall never die. Believest thou this?
John 11:25, 26

Yet a little while, and the world seeth me no more; but ye see me: because I live, ye shall live also.   *John 14:19*

And with great power gave the apostles witness of the resurrection of the Lord Jesus: and great grace was upon them all.   *Acts 4:33*

REVENGE.

Dearly beloved, avenge not yourselves, but rather give place unto wrath: for it is written, Vengeance is mine; I will repay, saith the Lord. *Romans 12:19*

Do not gloat when your enemy falls; when he stumbles, do not let your heart rejoice . . . .
Proverbs 24:17 (NIV)

For we know him who said, "It is mine to avenge; I will repay." And again, "The Lord will judge his people." It is a dreadful thing to fall into the hands of the living God. *Hebrews 10:30, 31* (NIV)

"You have heard that it was said, 'Eye for eye, and tooth for tooth.' But I tell you, Do not resist an evil person. If someone strikes you on the right cheek, turn to him the other also. And if someone wants to sue you and take your tunic, let him have your cloak as well." *Matthew 5:38-41* (NIV)

For if you forgive men when they sin against you,

your heavenly Father will also forgive you.
Matthew 6:14 (NIV)

Do not seek revenge or bear a grudge against one of your people, but love your neighbor as yourself. I am the LORD.   *Leviticus 19:18* (NIV)

"It is mine to avenge: I will repay. In due time their foot will slip; their day of disaster is near and their doom rushes upon them."
Deuteronomy 32:35 (NIV)

I will make mine arrows drunk with blood, and my sword shall devour flesh; and that with the blood of the slain and of the captives, from the beginning of revenges upon the enemy.
Deuteronomy 32:42

See that none render evil for evil unto any man; but ever follow that which is good, both among yourselves, and to all men.   *1 Thessalonians 5:15*

salvation.

The LORD is my strength and song, and he is become my salvation: he is my God . . . and I will exalt him. *Exodus 15:2*

And say ye, Save us, O God of our salvation, and gather us together, and deliver us from the heathen, that we may give thanks to thy holy name, and glory in thy praise. *1 Chronicles 16:35*

Nevertheless, he saved them for his name's sake, that he might make his mighty power to be known.
Psalm 106:8

And as Moses lifted up the serpent in the wilderness, even so must the Son of man be lifted up: That whosoever believeth in him should not perish, but have eternal life. *John 3:14, 15*

. . . Jesus stood and cried, saying, If any man thirst, let him come unto me, and drink. He that believeth on me, as the scripture hath said, out of

his belly shall flow rivers of living water.
John 7:37, 38

Seek ye the LORD while he may be found, call ye upon him while he is near .... *Isaiah 55:6*

... To day if ye will hear his voice, harden not your hearts, as in the provocation, in the day of temptation in the wilderness ....
Hebrews 3:7, 8

Therefore if any man be in Christ, he is a new creature: old things are passed away; behold, all things are become new.   *2 Corinthians 5:17*

"... Salvation belongs to our God, who sits on the throne, and to the Lamb."
Revelation 7:10 (NIV)

"Here I am! I stand at the door and knock. If anyone hears my voice and opens the door, I will come in and eat with him, and he with me. To him who overcomes, I will give the right to sit with me on my throne, just as I overcame and sat down with my Father on his throne."
Revelation 3:20, 21 (NIV)

satan.

Thou art the anointed cherub that covereth; and I have set thee so: thou wast upon the holy mountain of God; thou hast walked up and down in the midst of the stones of fire. Thou wast perfect in thy ways from the day that thou wast created, till iniquity was found in thee.   *Ezekiel 28:14, 15*

How art thou fallen from heaven, O Lucifer, son of the morning! how art thou cut down to the ground, which didst weaken the nations! For thou hast said in thine heart, I will ascend into heaven, I will exalt my throne above the stars of God . . . I will be like the most High. Yet thou shalt be brought down to hell, to the sides of the pit. They that see thee shall narrowly look upon thee, and consider thee saying, Is this the man that made the earth to tremble, that did shake kingdoms . . . .   *Isaiah 14:12-16*

Be sober, be vigilant; because your adversary the devil, as a roaring lion, walketh about, seeking whom he may devour . . . .   *1 Peter 5:8*

But if our gospel be hid, it is hid to them that are lost: In whom the god of this world hath blinded the minds of them which believe not, lest the light of the glorious gospel of Christ, who is the image of God, shall shine unto them.
2 Corinthians 4:3, 4

Ye are of your father the devil, and the lusts of your father ye will do. He was a murderer from the beginning, and abode not in the truth, because there is not truth in him. When he speaketh a lie, he speaketh of his own: for he is a liar, and the father of it. *John 8:44*

Put on the whole armour of God, that ye may be able to stand against the wiles of the devil.
Ephesians 6:11

. . . Satan himself masquerades as an angel of light. *2 Corinthians 11:14* (NIV)

But we see Jesus, who was made a little lower than the angels for the suffering of death, crowned with glory and honour; that he by the grace of God should taste death for every man . . . that through death he might destroy him that had the power of death, that is, the devil; and deliver them who through fear of death were all their lifetime subject to bondage. *Hebrews 2:9, 14, 15*

And the great dragon was cast out, that old serpent, called the Devil, and Satan, which deceiveth the whole world: he was cast out into the earth, and his angels were cast out with him. And I heard a loud voice saying in heaven, Now is come salvation, and strength, and the kingdom of our God, and the power of his Christ: for the accuser of our brethren is cast down, which accused them before our God day and night. And they overcame him by the blood of the Lamb, and by the word of their testimony; and they loved not their lives unto the death. *Revelation 12:9-11*

And the devil that deceived them was cast into the lake of fire and brimstone, where the beast and the false prophet are, and shall be tormented day and night for ever and ever. *Revelation 20:10*

SELF-CONTROL.

A fool gives full vent to his anger, but a wise man keeps himself under control.
Proverbs 29:11 (NIV)

But the fruit of the Spirit is love, joy, peace, patience, kindness, goodness, faithfulness, gentleness, and self-control. Against such things there is no law. *Galatians 5:22, 23* (NIV)

For this very reason, make every effort to add to your faith goodness, and to goodness, knowledge; and to knowledge, self-control; and to self-control, perseverance; and to perseverance, godliness; and to godliness, brotherly kindness, and to brotherly kindness, love. For if you possess these qualities in increasing measure, they will keep you from being ineffective and unproductive in your knowledge of our Lord Jesus Christ. *2 Peter 1:5-8* (NIV)

But I keep under my body, and bring it into subjection: lest that by any means, when I have

preached to others, I myself should be a castaway.
1 Corinthians 9:27

Judge me, O LORD: for I have walked in mine integrity: I have trusted also in the LORD, therefore I shall not slide. Examine me, O LORD and prove me; try my reins and my heart.
Psalm 26:1, 2

Finally, my brethren, be strong in the Lord, and in the power of his might. Put on the whole armour of God, that ye may be able to stand against the wiles of the devil. For we wrestle not against flesh and blood, but against principalities, against powers, against the rulers of the darkness of this world, against spiritual wickedness in high places.
Ephesians 6:10-12

Have nothing to do with godless myths and old wives' tales; rather, train yourself to be godly. For physical training is of some value, but godliness has value for all things, holding promise for both the present life and the life to come.
1 Timothy 4:7, 8 (NIV)

Blessed is the man that endureth temptation: for when he is tried, he shall receive the crown of life, which the Lord hath promised to them that love him. *James 1:12*

self-image.

I praise you because I am fearfully and wonderfully made; your works are wonderful, I know that full well. My frame was not hidden from you when I was made in the secret place. When I was woven together in the depths of the earth, your eyes saw my unformed body. All the days ordained for me were written in your book before one of them came to be.   *Psalm 139:14-16* (NIV)

For we are his workmanship, created in Christ Jesus unto good works, which God hath before ordained that we should walk in them.
Ephesians 2:10

And God said, Let us make man in our image, after our likeness . . . So God created man in his own image, in the image of God created he him; male and female created he them.   *Genesis 1:26, 27*

For the LORD shall be thy confidence, and shall keep thy foot from being taken.   *Proverbs 3:26*

For those God foreknew he also predestined to be conformed to the likeness of his Son, that he might be the firstborn among many brothers.
Romans 8:29 (NIV)

I am the vine, ye are the branches: he that abideth in me, and I in him, the same bringeth forth much fruit: for without me ye can do nothing. *John 15:5*

These things have I spoken unto you, that my joy might remain in you, and that your joy might be full. *John 15:11*

For as he thinketh in his heart, so is he . . . .
Proverbs 23:7

self-pity.

My tears have been my meat day and night, while they continually say unto me, where is thy God?   *Psalm 42:3*

... The LORD came to him, and said he unto him, What doest thou here, Elijah? And he said, I have been very jealous for the LORD God of hosts: for the children of Israel have forsaken thy covenant, thrown down thine altars, and slain thy prophets with the sword; and I, even I only, am left; and they seek my life, to take it away.   *1 Kings 29:10*

... He himself went a day's journey into the desert. He came to a broom tree, sat down under it and prayed that he might die. "I have had enough, LORD," he said. "Take my life; I am no better than my ancestors." *1 Kings 19:4* (NIV)

And Job spake, and said, Let the day perish wherein I was born, and the night in which it was said, There is a man child conceived.   *Job 3:1, 2*

ARMED AND DANGEROUS

And Moses said unto the LORD, O my Lord, I am not eloquent . . . but I am slow of speech, and of a slow tongue. And the LORD said unto him, Who hath made man's mouth? or who maketh the dumb, or deaf, or the seeing, or the blind? have not I the LORD? Now therefore go, and I will be with thy mouth and teach thee what thou shalt say.
Exodus 4:10-12

For who makes you different from anyone else? What do you have that you did not receive? and if you did receive it, why do you boast as though you did not? *1 Corinthians 4:7* (NIV)

. . . Ye were not redeemed with corruptible things, as silver and gold . . . But with the precious blood of Christ . . . . *1 Peter 1:18, 19*

For I was envious at the foolish, when I saw the prosperity of the wicked. Verily I have cleansed my heart in vain, and washed my hands in innocency. For all the day long have I been plagued, and chastened every morning. When I thought to know this, it was too painful for me; until I went into the sanctuary of God; then understood I their end.
Psalm 73:3, 13, 14, 16, 17

SEXUAL IMMORALITY.

Flee from sexual immorality. All other sins a man commits are outside his body, but he who sins sexually sins against his own body.
1 Corinthians 6:18 (NIV)

For this is the will of God, even your sanctification, that ye should abstain from fornication: That every one of you should know how to possess his vessel in sanctification and honour . . . For God has not called us unto uncleanness, but unto holiness. *1 Thessalonians 4:3, 4, 7*

Marriage should be honored by all, and the marriage bed kept pure, for God will judge the adulterer and all the sexually immoral. *Hebrews 13:4* (NIV)

You have heard that it was said by them of old time, thou shalt not commit adultery: But I say unto you, That whosoever looketh on a woman to lust after her hath committed adultery with her already in his heart. *Matthew 5:27, 28*

The acts of the sinful nature are obvious: sexual immorality, impurity and debauchery . . . and envy; drunkenness, orgies, and the like. I warn you, as I did before, that those who live like this will not inherit the kingdom of God. *Galatians 5:19, 21* (NIV)

What? Know ye not that your body is the temple of the Holy Ghost which is in you, which ye have of God, and ye are not your own? For ye are bought with a price: therefore glorify God in your body, and in your spirit, which are God's.
1 Corinthians 6:19, 20

But since there is so much immorality, each man should have his own wife, and each woman her own husband . . . Now to the unmarried and the widows I say: It is good for them to stay unmarried, as I am. But if they cannot control themselves, they should marry, for it is better to marry than to burn with passion. *1 Corinthians 7:2, 8, 9* (NIV)

The Lord knoweth how to deliver the godly out of temptations, and to reserve the unjust unto the day of judgment to be punished . . . . *2 Peter 2:9*

No temptation has seized you except what is common to man. And God is faithful; he will not let you be tempted beyond what you can bear. But when you are tempted, he will provide a way out so that you can stand up under it.
1 Corinthians 10:13 (NIV)

shame.

... I fell upon my knees, and spread out my hands unto the LORD my God, and said, O my God, I am ashamed and blush to lift up my face to thee, my God: for our iniquities are increased over our head, and our trespass is grown up into the heavens.
Ezra 9:5, 6

But he was wounded for our transgressions, he was bruised for our iniquities . . . and with his stripes we are healed.   *Isaiah 53:5*

As it is written, Behold, I lay in Sion a stumblingstone and rock of offence: and whosoever believeth on him shall not be ashamed.   *Romans 9:33*

Fear not; for thou shalt not be ashamed: neither be thou confounded; for thou shalt not be put to shame: for thou shalt forget the shame of thy youth, and shalt not remember the reproach of thy widowhood any more. For thy Maker is thine husband; the LORD of hosts is his name; and thy Redeemer the Holy One of Israel; the God of the whole earth shall he be called. *Isaiah 54:4, 5*

... In you I trust, O my God. Do not let me be put to shame, nor let my enemies triumph over me. No one whose hope is in you will ever be put to shame, but they will be put to shame who are treacherous without excuse. *Psalm 25:2, 3* (NIV)

For the scripture saith, Whosoever believeth on him shall not be ashamed. *Romans 10:11*

talents.

And I was afraid, and went and hid thy talent in the earth: lo, there thou hast that is thine. His lord answered and said unto him, Thou wicked and slothful servant . . . Take therefore the talent from him, and give it unto him which hath ten talents. For unto every one that hath shall be given, and he shall have abundance: but from him that hath not shall be taken away even that which he hath. And cast ye the unprofitable servant into outer darkness: there shall be weeping and gnashing of teeth.
Matthew 25:25, 26, 28-30

A man's gift maketh room for him, and bringeth him before great men.   *Proverbs 18:16*

. . . For God's gifts and his call are irrevocable.
Romans 11:29 (NIV)

Having then gifts differing according to the grace that is given to us, whether prophecy, let us prophesy according to the proportion of faith; or ministry, let us wait on our ministering: or he that teacheth, on teaching; or he that exhorteth, on exhortation: he that giveth, let him do it with simplicity; he that ruleth, with diligence; he that sheweth mercy, with cheerfulness.   *Romans 12:6-8*

... For unto whomsoever much is given, of him shall be much required: and to whom men have committed much, of him they will ask more.
Luke 12:48

TEMPTATION.

And Jesus answered and said unto him, Get thee behind me, Satan: for it is written, Thou shalt worship the Lord thy God, and him only shalt thou serve.   *Luke 4:8*

There hath no temptation taken you but such as is common to man: but God is faithful, who will not suffer you to be tempted above that ye are able; but will with the temptation also make a way to escape, that ye may be able to bear it.
1 Corinthians 10:13

Finally, my brethren, be strong in the Lord, and in the power of his might. Put on the whole armour of God that ye may be able to stand against the wiles of the devil. For we wrestle not against flesh and blood, but against principalities, against powers, against the rulers of the darkness of this world, against spiritual wickedness in high places.
Ephesians 6:10-12

Knowing this, that the trying of your faith worketh patience. But let patience have her perfect work, that ye may be perfect and entire, wanting nothing.
James 1:2-4

The Lord knoweth how to deliver the godly out of temptations, and to preserve the unjust unto the day of judgement to be punished . . . *2 Peter 2:9*

Blessed is the man that endureth temptation: for when he is tried, he shall receive the crown of life, which the Lord hath promised to them that love him. Let no man say when he is tempted, I am tempted of God: for God cannot be tempted with evil, neither tempteth he any man: Then when lust hath conceived, it bringeth forth sin: and sin, when it is finished, bringeth forth death.
James 1:12, 13, 15

My son, if sinners entice thee, consent thou not.
Proverbs 1:12

Watch and pray, that ye enter not into temptation: the spirit indeed is willing, but the flesh is weak.
Matthew 26:41

And when he was at the place, he said unto them, Pray that ye enter not into temptation. *Luke 22:40*

Because thou hast kept the word of my patience, I also will keep thee from the hour of temptation, which shall come upon all the world, to try them that dwell upon the earth.   *Revelation 3:10*

For in that he himself hath suffered being tempted, he is able to succour them that are tempted.
Hebrews 2:18

For we have not an high priest which cannot be touched with the feeling of our infirmities; but was in all points tempted like as we are, yet without sin.
Hebrews 4:15

These things I have spoken unto you, that in me ye might have peace. In the world ye shall have tribulation: but be of good cheer; I have overcome the world.   *John 16:33*

thankfulness.

I thank my God upon every remembrance of you, always in every prayer of mine for you all making request with joy, for your fellowship in the gospel from the first day until now . . . .
Philippians 1:1-3

In everything give thanks: for this is the will of God in Christ Jesus concerning you.
1 Thessalonians 5:18

Let us come before his presence with thanksgiving, and make a joyful noise unto him with psalms.
Psalm 95:2

Enter his gates with thanksgiving, and into his courts with praise: be thankful unto him, and bless his name.   *Psalm 100:4*

O give thanks unto the LORD; call upon his name: make known his deeds among the people.
Psalm 105:1

232 Thankfulness

O give thanks unto the LORD; for he is good: because his mercy endureth for ever. *Psalm 118:1*

Giving thanks always for all things unto God and the Father in the name of our Lord Jesus Christ . . . .
Ephesians 5:20

Saying, Amen: Blessing, and glory, and wisdom, and thanksgiving, and honour, and power, and might, be unto our God for ever and ever. Amen.
Revelation 7:12

Oh give thanks unto the LORD; for he is good: for his mercy endureth for ever. *Psalm 136:1*

thoughts.

But those things which proceed out of the mouth come forth from the heart; and they defile the man. For out of the heart proceed evil thoughts, murders, adulteries, fornications, thefts, false witness, blasphemies . . . .   *Matthew 15:18, 19*

Set your affection on things above, not on things on the earth.   *Colossians 3:2*

And be not conformed to this world: but be ye transformed by the renewing of your mind, that ye may prove what is that good, and acceptable, and perfect will of God.   *Romans 12:2*

Let this mind be in you, which was also in Christ Jesus . . . .   *Philippians 2:5*

And herein do I exercise myself, to have always a conscience void of offence toward God, and toward men.   *Acts 24:16*

Finally, brethren, whatsoever things are true, whatsoever things are honest, whatsoever things are just, whatsoever things are pure, whatsoever things are lovely, whatsoever things are of good report; if there be any virtue, and if there by any praise, think on these things.   *Philippians 4:8*

The wicked, through the pride of his countenance, will not seek after God: God is not in all his thoughts.   *Psalm 10:4*

The LORD knoweth the thoughts of man, that they are vanity.   *Psalm 94:11*

For my thoughts are not your thoughts, neither are your ways my ways, saith the LORD.   *Isaiah 55:8*

But when they shall lead you, and deliver you up, take no thought beforehand what ye shall speak, neither do ye premeditate: but whatsoever shall be given you in that hour, that speak ye: for it is not ye that speak, but the Holy Ghost.   *Mark 13:11*

Are ye not then partial in yourselves, and are become judges of evil thoughts?   *James 2:4*

Therefore I say unto you, Take no thought for your life, what ye shall eat, or what ye shall drink; nor yet for your body, what ye shall put on. Is not the life more than meat, and the body than raiment?
Matthew 6:25

TROUBLE.

The LORD also will be a refuge for the oppressed, a refuge in times of trouble.   *Psalm 9:9*

For in the time of trouble he shall hide me in his pavilion: in the secret of his tabernacle shall he hide me; he shall set me up upon a rock.   *Psalm 27:5*

I will be glad and rejoice in thy mercy: for thou has considered my trouble; thou hast known my soul in adversities . . . Have mercy upon me, O Lord, for I am in trouble: mine eye is consumed with grief, yea, my soul and my belly.
Psalm 31:7, 9

Cast thy burden upon the LORD, and he shall sustain thee: he shall never suffer the righteous to be moved.   *Psalm 55:22*

But the salvation of the righteous is of the LORD: he is their strength in the time of trouble. And the LORD shall help them, and deliver them: he shall deliver them from the wicked, and save them, because they trust in him. *Psalm 39:39, 40*

God is our refuge and strength, a very present help in trouble. *Psalm 46:1*

The righteous is delivered out of trouble, and the wicked cometh in his stead. *Psalm 11:8*

The LORD is my rock and my fortress, and my deliverer; my God, my strength, in whom I will trust; my buckler, and the horn of my salvation, and my high tower. *Psalm 18:2, 3*

Though I walk in the midst of trouble, thou wilt revive me: thou shalt stretch forth thine hand against the wrath of mine enemies, and thy right hand shall save me. The LORD will perfect that which concerneth me: thy mercy, O LORD, endureth for ever: forsake not the works of thine own hands.
Psalm 138:7, 8

Blessed be God, even the Father of our Lord Jesus Christ, the Father of mercies, and the God of all comfort; who comforteth us in all our tribulation, that we may be able to comfort them which are in any trouble, by the comfort wherewith we ourselves are comforted of God. *2 Corinthians 1:3, 4*

Peace I leave with you, my peace I give unto you: not as the world giveth, give I unto you. Let not your heart be troubled, neither let it be afraid.
John 14:27

trust.

Trust in the LORD with all thine heart; and lean not unto thine own understanding. In all thy ways acknowledge him, and he shall direct thy paths.
Proverbs 3:5, 6

Though he slay me, yet will I trust in him: but I will maintain mine own ways before him.
Job 13:15

O LORD my God, in thee do I put my trust: save me from all them that persecute me, and deliver me . . . . *Psalm 7:1*

Nay, in all these things we are more than conquerors through him that loved us. *Romans 8:37*

The God of my rock; in him will I trust: he is my shield, and the horn of my salvation, my high tower, and my refuge, my saviour; thou savest me from violence. *2 Samuel 22:3*

Offer the sacrifices of righteousness, and put your trust in the LORD. *Psalm 4:5*

Some trust in chariots, and some in horses: but we will remember the name of the LORD our God.
Psalm 20:7

They that trust in their wealth, and boast themselves in the multitude of their riches; none of them can by any means redeem his brother, nor give to God a ransom for him . . . . *Psalm 49:6, 7*

Trust in the LORD, and do good; so shalt thou dwell in the land, and verily thou shalt be fed. Delight thyself also in the LORD; and he shall give the desires of thine heart. Commit thy way unto the LORD; trust also in him; and he shall bring it to pass. *Psalm 37:3-5*

Every word of God is pure: he is a shield unto them that put their trust in him. *Proverbs 30:5*

unpardonable sin.

The unpardonable sin is simply defined as giving Satan the glory for work done by the Holy Spirit.

He that is not with me is against me; and he that gathereth not with me scattereth abroad. Wherefore I say unto you, All manner of sin and blasphemy shall be forgiven unto men: but the blasphemy against the Holy Ghost shall not be forgiven unto men. And whosoever speaketh a word against the Son of man, it shall be forgiven him: but whosoever speaketh against the Holy Ghost, it shall not be forgiven him, neither in this world, neither in the world to come.   *Matthew 12:31, 32*

For it is impossible for those who were once enlightened, and have tasted of the heavenly gift, and were made partakers of the Holy Ghost, and have tasted the good word of God, and the powers of the world to come, if they shall fall away, to renew them again unto repentance; seeing they crucify to themselves the Son of God afresh, and put him to an open shame.   *Hebrews 6:4-6*

For if after they have escaped the pollutions of the world through the knowledge of the Lord and Saviour Jesus Christ, they are again entangled therein, and overcome, the latter end is worse with them than the beginning.   *2 Peter 2:20*

If we deliberately keep on sinning after we have received the knowledge of the truth, no sacrifice for sins is left, but only a fearful expectation of judgment and of raging fire that will consume the enemies of God. Anyone who rejected the law of Moses died without mercy on the testimony of two or three witnesses. How much more severely do you think a man deserves to be punished who has trampled the Son of God under foot, who has treated as an unholy thing the blood of the covenant that sanctified him, and who has insulted the Spirit of grace?   *Hebrews 10:26-29* (NIV)

The Lord is not slack concerning his promise, as some men count slackness; but is longsuffering to us-ward, not willing that any should perish, but that all should come to repentance.   *2 Peter 3:9*

WAR.

From whence come wars and fightings among you? come they not hence, even of your lusts that war in your members? Ye lust, and have not: ye kill and desire to have, and cannot obtain: ye fight and war, yet have not, because ye ask not. Ye ask, and receive not, because ye ask amiss, that ye may consume it upon your lusts.   *James 4:1-3*

I urge, then, first of all, that requests, prayers, intercession and thanksgiving be made for everyone—for kings and all those in authority, that we may live peaceful and quiet lives in all godliness and holiness.   *1 Timothy 2:1, 2* (NIV)

Blessed are the peacemakers: for they shall be called the children of God.   *Matthew 5:9*

To every thing there is a season, and a time to every purpose under heaven . . . A time to kill, and a time to heal; a time to break down, and a time

to build up . . . A time to love, and a time to hate; a time of war, and a time of peace.
Ecclesiastes 3:1, 2, 8

For rulers are not a terror to good works, but to the evil. Wilt thou then not be afraid of power? do that which is good, and thou shalt have praise of the same.   *Romans 13:3*

Submit yourselves to every ordinance of man for the Lord's sake: whether it be to the king, as supreme; or unto governors, as unto them that are sent by him for the punishment of evildoers, and for the praise of them that do well.
1 Peter 2:13, 14

And he shall judge among the nations, and shall rebuke many people: and they shall beat their swords into plowshares, and their spears into pruninghooks: nation shall not lift up sword against nation, neither shall they learn war any more.   *Isaiah 2:4*

will of God.
(how to find, know, and obey)

Commit to the LORD whatever you do, and your plans will succeed.   *Proverbs 16:3 (NIV)*

I delight to do thy will, O my God: yea, thy law is within my heart.   *Psalm 40:8*

Hath the LORD as great delight in burnt offerings and sacrifices, as in obeying the voice of the LORD? Behold, to obey is better than sacrifice, and to hearken than the fat of rams.   *1 Samuel 15:22*

Thy word is a lamp unto my feet, and a light unto my path.   *Psalm 119:105*

I, being in the way, the LORD led me.
Genesis 27:24

Howbeit when he, the Spirit of truth, is come, he will guide you into all truth: for he shall not speak of himself; but whatsoever he shall hear, that shall he speak: and he will shew you things to come.   *John 16:13*

For the LORD God is a sun and shield: the LORD will give grace and glory: no good thing will he withhold from them that walk uprightly.
Psalm 84:11

I will instruct thee and teach thee in the way which thou shalt go: I will guide thee with mine eye. Be ye not as the horse, or as the mule, which have no understanding: whose mouth must be held in with bit and bridle, lest they come near unto thee.
Psalm 32:8, 9

Cause me to hear thy lovingkindness in the morning; for in thee do I trust: cause me to know the way wherein I should walk; for I lift up my soul unto thee.   *Psalm 143:8*

Thy kingdom come. Thy will be done in earth, as it is in heaven.   *Matthew 6:10*

Not every one that saith unto me, Lord, Lord, shall enter into the kingdom of heaven; but he that doeth the will of my Father which is in heaven.
Matthew 7:21

In every thing give thanks: for this is the will of God in Christ Jesus concerning you.
1 Thessalonians 5:18

Shew me thy ways, O LORD: teach me thy paths. Lead me in thy truth, and teach me: for thou art the God of my salvation; on thee do I wait all the day. *Psalm 25:4, 5*

If you love me keep my commandments . . . If a man love me, he will keep my words: and my Father will love him, and we will come unto him, and make our abode with him. *John 14:15, 23*

wisdom.

The fear of the LORD is the beginning of knowledge: but fools despise wisdom and instruction.
Proverbs 1:7

Blessed is the man that walketh not in the counsel of the ungodly, nor standeth in the way of sinners, nor sitteth in the seat of the scornful. But his delight is in the law of the LORD; and in his law doth meditate day and night. *Psalm 1:1, 2*

Happy is the man that findeth wisdom, and the man that getteth understanding. *Proverbs 3:3*

For the LORD giveth wisdom: out of his mouth cometh knowledge and understanding.
Proverbs 2:6

Behold, thou desirest truth in the inward parts: and in the hidden part thou shalt make me to know wisdom. *Psalm 51:6*

Wisdom

If any of you lack wisdom, let him ask of God, that giveth to all men liberally, and upbraideth not; and it shall be given him.   *James 1:5*

Let the word of Christ dwell in you richly in all wisdom; teaching and admonishing one another in psalms and hymns and spiritual songs, singing with grace in your hearts to the Lord.   *Colossians 3:16*

WITNESSING.

For I am not ashamed of the gospel of Christ: for it is the power of God unto salvation to every one that believeth . . . .   *Romans 1:16*

But ye shall receive power, after that the Holy Ghost is come upon you: and ye shall be witnesses unto me both in Jerusalem, and in all Judea, and in Samaria, and unto the uttermost part of the earth.
Acts 1:8

Go ye into all the world, and preach the gospel to every creature. He that believeth and is baptized shall be saved: but he that believeth not shall be damned.   *Mark 16:15, 16*

Go ye therefore, and teach all nations, baptizing them in the name of the Father, and of the Son, and of the Holy Ghost: Teaching them to observe all things whatsoever I have commanded you: and, lo, I am with you alway, even unto the end of the world. Amen.   *Matthew 28:19, 20*

Witnessing

Because of the service by which you have proved yourselves, men will praise God for the obedience that accompanies your confession of the gospel of Christ, and for your generosity in sharing with them and with everyone else. *2 Corinthians 9:13* (NIV)

... Do the work of an evangelist, make full proof of thy ministry. *2 Timothy 4:5*

For whosoever shall call upon the name of the Lord shall be saved. How then shall they call on him in whom they have not believed? and how shall they believe in him of whom they have not heard? and how shall they hear without a preacher?
Romans 10:13, 14

Now when they saw the boldness of Peter and John, and perceived that they were unlearned and ignorant men, they marvelled; and they took knowledge of them, that they had been with Jesus. *Acts 4:13*

But sanctify the Lord God in your hearts: and be ready always to give an answer to every man that asketh you a reason of the hope that is in you . . . .
1 Peter 3:15

These Scriptures will help you as you share your faith in Jesus Christ with others. Commit the verses to memory so you will always be ready to give a reason for the hope that is in you (*1 Peter 3:15*).

John 3:16	John 1:12
1 John 4:10	John 14:6
Romans 3:10	Acts 3:19
Romans 3:23	Acts 16:31
Romans 6:23	1 John 1:9
Romans 10:9-11	John 3:36
Galatians 2:16	2 Corinthians 5:17

Philippians 4:3

work.

The laborer's appetite works for him; his hunger drives him on.   *Proverbs 16:26* (NIV)

Do you see a man skilled in his work? He will serve before kings; he will not serve before obscure men.   *Proverbs 22:29* (NIV)

For even when we were with you, this we commanded you, that if any would not work, neither should he eat.   *2 Thessalonians 3:10*

But if any provide not for his own, and specially for those of his own house, he hath denied the faith, and is worse than an infidel.   *1 Timothy 5:8*

Every man's work shall be made manifest: for the day shall declare it, because it shall be revealed by fire; and the fire shall try every man's work of what sort it is. If any man's work abide which he hath built thereupon, he shall receive a reward. If any man's work shall be burned, he shall suffer loss;

but he himself shall be saved; yet so as by fire.
1 Corinthians 3:13-15

And whatsoever ye do in word or deed, do all in the name of the Lord Jesus, giving thanks to God and the Father by him . . . And whatsoever ye do, do it heartily, as to the Lord, and not unto men; knowing that of the Lord, ye shall receive the reward of the inheritance: for ye serve the Lord Christ.   *Colossians 3:17, 23, 24*

worship.

For thou shalt worship no other god: for the LORD, whose name is Jealous, is a jealous God . . . . *Exodus 34:13*

Give unto the LORD the glory due unto his name; worship the LORD in the beauty of holiness.
Psalm 29:2

Then saith Jesus unto him, Get thee hence, Satan: for it is written, Thou shalt worship the Lord thy God, and him only shalt thou serve. Then the devil leaveth him, and, behold, angels came and ministered unto him. *Matthew 4:10,11*

O come, let us worship and bow down: let us kneel before the LORD our maker. *Psalm 95:6*

Enter into his gates with thanksgiving, and into his courts with praise: be thankful unto him, and bless his name. *Psalm 100:4*

ARMED AND DANGEROUS 255

But the hour cometh, and now is, when the true worshippers shall worship the Father in spirit and in truth: for the Father seeketh such to worship him. God is a Spirit: and they that worship him must worship him in spirit and in truth.   *John 4:23, 24*

O sing unto the LORD a new song: sing unto the LORD, all the earth . . . For the LORD is great, and greatly to be praised: he is to be feared above all gods . . . Honour and majesty are before him: strength and beauty are in his sanctuary . . . Give unto the LORD the glory due unto his name: bring an offering, and come into his courts. O worship the LORD in the beauty of holiness: fear before him, all the earth . . . Let the heavens rejoice, and let the earth be glad; let the sea roar, and the fulness thereof.   *Psalm 96:1, 4, 6, 8, 9,11*

Holy, holy, holy, Lord God Almighty, which was, and is, and is to come.   *Revelation 4:8*

The four and twenty elders fall down before him that sat on the throne, and worship him that liveth for ever and ever, and cast their crowns before the throne, saying, Thou art worthy, O Lord, to receive glory and honour and all power: for thou hast created all things, and for thy pleasure they are and were created.   *Revelation 4:10, 11*

Worship

Then I looked and heard the voice of many angels, numbering thousands upon thousands, and ten thousand times ten thousand. They encircled the throne and the living creatures and the elders. In a loud voice they sang: "Worthy is the Lamb, who was slain, to receive power and wealth and wisdom and strength and honor and glory and praise!" Then I heard every creature in heaven and on earth and under the earth and on the sea, and all that is in them, singing: "To him who sits on the throne and to the Lamb be praise and honor and glory and power, for ever and ever!" The four living creatures said, "Amen," and the elders fell down and worshiped.

Revelation 5:11-14 (NIV)

Favorite Scriptures

Favorite Scriptures

Favorite Scriptures